READING MARK

CASCADE COMPANIONS

The Christian theological tradition provides an embarrassment of riches: from Scripture to modern scholarship, we are blessed with a vast and complex theological inheritance. And yet this feast of traditional riches is too frequently inaccessible to the general reader.

The Cascade Companions series addresses the challenge by publishing books that combine academic rigor with broad appeal and readability. They aim to introduce nonspecialist readers to that vital storehouse of authors, documents, themes, histories, arguments, and movements that comprise this heritage with brief yet compelling volumes.

READING MARK

KELLY R. IVERSON

CASCADE *Books* • Eugene, Oregon

READING MARK
Cascade Companions

Cascade Books
An Imprint of Wipf and Stock Publishers
199 W. 8th Ave., Suite 3
Eugene, OR 97401

www.wipfandstock.com

PAPERBACK ISBN: 978-1-4982-3002-5
HARDCOVER ISBN: 978-1-4982-3004-9
EBOOK ISBN: 978-1-4982-3003-2

Cataloguing-in-Publication data:

Names: Iverson, Kelly R., author.

Title: Reading Mark / Kelly R. Iverson.

Description: Eugene, OR: Cascade Books, 2023. | Cascade Companions. | Includes bibliographical references.

Identifiers: ISBN 978-1-4982-3002-5 (paperback). | ISBN 978-1-4982-3004-9 (hardcover). | ISBN 978-1-4982-3003-2 (ebook).

Subjects: LSCH: Bible—Mark—Criticism, interpretation, etc. | Bible. Gospels—Criticism, interpretation, etc.

Classification: BS2585.2 I 94 2023 (print). | BS2585.2 (ebook).

VERSION NUMBER 09/25/23

To Caleb, Peyton, and Jada . . .
Our hearts follow wherever you go

CONTENTS

ABBREVIATIONS

AB	Anchor Bible
BBR	*Bulletin for Biblical Research*
Bib	*Biblica*
BIS	Biblical Interpretation Series
BNTC	Black's New Testament Commentaries
BPCS	Biblical Performance Criticism Series
CBQ	*Catholic Biblical Quarterly*
IRT	Issues in Religion and Theology
JBL	*Journal of Biblical Literature*
JETS	*Journal of the Evangelical Theological Society*
JR	*Journal of Religion*
JSNT	*Journal for the Study of the New Testament*
JSNTSup	Journal for the Study of the New Testament Supplement Series
JSOT	*Journal for the Study of the Old Testament*
JTS	*Journal of Theological Studies*
JTSA	*Journal of Theology for Southern Africa*
LNTS	Library of New Testament Studies

LXX	Septuagint
MS/MSS	Manuscript(s)
NIGTC	New International Greek Testament Commentary
NovT	*Novum Testamentum*
NRSV	New Revised Standard Version
NT	New Testament
NTL	New Testament Library
OT	Old Testament
SBL	Society of Biblical Literature
SNTSMS	Society for New Testament Studies Monograph Series
SP	Sacra Pagina
WBC	Word Biblical Commentary
WUNT	Wissenschaftliche Untersuchungen zum Neuen Testament

1

PRELIMINARY CONSIDERATIONS

I STILL REMEMBER TAKING my first course in the Gospels. Like many, I was acquainted with the stories of healing and teaching, death and resurrection found in the Gospel traditions. I had read the Gospels and learned about them in church. And I assumed that this course would supplement my understanding, given my perceived familiarity with the Gospels. I did not anticipate, however, how genuinely transformative the experience would be. Yes, Jesus was our primary subject matter, and yes, the Gospels were the locus of our discussion. But this class was different. Time and again, the questions and concepts raised in the course were completely new or beyond my consideration. As the days and weeks stacked on top of one another, I felt awestruck— as though I was reading the Gospels for the first time. It was as if scales fell from my eyes (cf. Acts 9:18) revealing an exciting world of interpretive possibilities and questions to be explored. Though the experience was strange and unfamiliar in certain respects, and perhaps even disconcerting at times, any apprehension paled in comparison to the intrigue and excitement that challenged my understanding. The experience was so enriching and stimulating—indeed, I am still studying the Gospels today—I wondered why I had not been introduced to these discussions long before.

This book is designed, in part, to fill this gap—to guide learners into this new and fascinating world of discovery and to acquaint them with the Gospel of Mark. It is intended for undergraduates, lay people, or anyone pursing an introductory study of Mark. As a guide, it is not meant to provide an exhaustive analysis or a verse-by-verse interpretation of Mark. Rather the book highlights various issues that are central to an appreciation of Mark's narrative. While drawing attention to the scenic landmarks and noteworthy discussions along the way, the aim is to make the best of scholarly discussion available in a nontechnical, easy-to-read format. As such, this book is not encumbered by extensive notes and scholarly citations, even though it is informed by the work of countless others. The overarching goal is to introduce students to the narrative of Mark's Gospel with the hope that it stimulates a greater sense of wonderment for the beauty and complexity of the text and for the One who stands behind and before the second Gospel.

Before launching into a formal examination of Mark's narrative, it is important to consider seven issues that undergird the study. These background issues, ranging from questions of authorship and genre to methodological approach, can be complex and contested. While there will be no attempt to resolve these matters, a rudimentary appreciation is necessary. Indeed, all interpreters should have some familiarity with these matters as they inform the broader interpretation of Mark.

(1) AUTHORSHIP

The second Gospel has traditionally been understood to have been written by "Mark." This Mark is assumed to be the John Mark of Acts, a Jewish man who lived in Jerusalem and was a follower of Jesus during the first century. According to Luke, Peter went to the home of Mark's mother after being miraculously led out of prison by an angel (Acts 12:4–17). The same John Mark is described as accompanying Paul and Barnabas on their first missionary journey (Acts 12:25; 13:4), before abandoning them at Perga (for unknown reasons) and returning to Jerusalem (Acts 13:13). Sometime later, when Paul and Barnabas set out on their second missionary journey, the two engaged in a contentious discussion about whether or not to bring John Mark (Acts 15:37–38). Although Barnabas was in favor (perhaps motivated by the fact that Mark was his cousin? [Col 4:10]), Paul was unwilling to overlook Mark's previous actions and vigorously opposed his participation on the second missionary journey. The issue was so contested that Paul and Barnabas parted ways, with Barnabas taking John Mark and sailing to Cyprus, while Paul chose Silas for ministry in Asia Minor (Acts 15:39–40). Although Acts depicts a split, other NT texts suggest some form of reconciliation between Paul and Mark in the years thereafter (Col 4:10; Phlm 24; 2 Tim 4:11), and 1 Pet 5:13 places Mark in Rome alongside Peter and Silas (potentially during the period in which Paul was also in Rome).

This latter reference is particularly important in view of the fact that church tradition associates the Gospel of Mark with the apostle Peter. The first indication of this tradition comes from the second-century bishop Papias, whose writings are no longer available, but are nonetheless referenced in a fourth-century work by Eusebius, an early church historian. According to a tradition received by

Papias (Eusebius, *Eccl. hist.* 3.39.15), Mark is identified as an interpreter of Peter. Though Mark was not an eyewitness or companion of Jesus, he wrote as much as he remembered from the teachings of Peter. Papias suggests that the resulting Gospel, based on the testimony of Peter, was not necessarily in order or complete but nonetheless provides an accurate depiction of Jesus's ministry. Papias's account is noteworthy since it draws an explicit connection between the Gospel of Mark and the apostolic Peter, seemingly lending authority to the teachings of the second Gospel.

More recent scholarly discussion has questioned this assessment. To begin, it is widely acknowledged that the title of the Gospel ("The Gospel According to Mark") was a later addition to the text and is not original. The title itself occurs in various forms and at different places in different manuscripts: some at the beginning, end, or both. However, it likely did not originate until the late first or early second century. Technically speaking, the second Gospel is an anonymous account of the life and ministry of Jesus since nowhere does the author provide a note of self-identification.

The Gospel may have been written by a "Mark"—an extremely common name in the first century—but there is reason to consider whether this individual is the same John Mark of the NT and linked to Peter by Papias. Some have argued that the positive depiction of gentiles (e.g., 5:1–20; 7:24–30, 31–37; 8:1–9) and the geographical conundrums (5:1; 6:45, 53; 7:31) in the text are at odds with a supposedly Jewish author who was living in Jerusalem. Even the connection to Peter seems problematic. Had Peter's testimony been the driving impetus for the narrative, it is curious that Peter does not play a more prominent role in the text. Somewhat surprisingly, Peter plays a larger role in Matthew's Gospel, which includes several important traditions about

Peter that are not included in Mark's narrative (e.g., Matt 14:28–31; 16:17–19; 17:24–27). While none of these arguments are decisive, they expose the difficulty of answering this basic question about the author of the text. Fortunately, the message of the second Gospel does not hinge on the resolution to this issue. The remainder of the volume will continue to make use of the designation "Mark," even if it is not possible to pinpoint the exact identity of the author.

(2) SETTING

For whom and where was the Gospel of Mark written? Over the last hundred years, scholars have widely affirmed that the Gospels—including Mark—were written in and for particular communities of faith. A number of possibilities have been suggested for Mark, including Rome, Galilee, Jerusalem, and Syria. Each of these proposals represents a genuine possibility and is attractive in certain respects. Yet it is impossible to be certain since the recipients are nowhere identified within the text of Mark's Gospel. The best interpreters can do is make inferences about the audience based on the text itself. Though the evidence within the narrative makes it difficult to isolate a single geographic locale, what can be affirmed are certain characteristics of the community. On this point, there is far more agreement.

The evidence suggests that Mark was likely written for a community of Jews and gentiles (though predominately gentile) facing persecution. Scholars frequently point to Mark's tendency to translate Aramaic expressions (5:41; 7:34; 14:36; 15:22, 34) and to explain Jewish practices (2:19; 7:3–4; 10:2; 14:1, 12, 64; 15:42) for this primarily gentile audience. The text seems to imply that the community was likely facing some form of persecution and suffering. Besides the repeated emphasis on persecution and suffering

(8:34–38; 9:42–48; 10:17–31, 38–39), some have argued that the entire narrative is structured around these themes (4:16–17; 13:9–13) and therefore composed to address the community's own situation.

More recently, Richard Bauckham has challenged the view that the Gospels were written for particular communities. Bauckham has argued that the Gospels were for all churches and all Christians, not necessarily specific communities. He further suggests that the consensus view is a hypothesis that has never been adequately argued and that it confuses the communities in which the texts were composed with the audiences to whom they were written. Bauckham maintains that scholars have mistakenly treated the Gospels as if they were Pauline letters written for particular communities of faith. In support of this theory, he suggests that the ancient world was highly mobile (good roads, safe travel), that the church understood itself in a unified fashion, and that there was widespread communication between different Christian communities. Because the early Christian movement was an open network of churches, Bauckham argues that Mark (as well as Matthew, Luke, and John) likely wrote with a broad and inclusive outlook, rather than to a particular locale.

Bauckham's work has brought renewed attention to the question of Gospel communities even if his approach has not been widely accepted. Two points illustrate what some regard as a weakness of Bauckham's view. First, the fact that the Gospel of Mark was an anonymous text (before the titles were added) may indicate that it was originally composed for a local community. That is, because Mark was written in and to a particular community, no authorial citation was necessary since the writer was undoubtedly known by the community. Titles were required only after the Gospels began to circulate.

Second, Mark 15:21 makes reference to Simon of Cyrene, who carried Jesus's cross and was the "father of Alexander and Rufus." Though seemingly an irrelevant detail, this verse is particularly problematic for Bauckham's thesis since it suggests that Alexander and Rufus were known by the intended recipients. If Mark was written for all Christians, why does the author include this reference since it would have been lost on most audience members who would not have known Alexander or Rufus? To this point, it is telling that both Matthew (27:32) and Luke (23:26) omit the reference to Alexander and Rufus. While it is true that Mark was eventually distributed to "all Christians," it seems likely that the Gospel was originally composed for a particular community of believers.

(3) DATE

Similar to questions of authorship and setting, the Markan composer does not provide an explicit indication of when the text was written. This does not mean, however, that there are no details that potentially suggest when to date the narrative. As a broad frame of reference, it seems obvious that the second Gospel must have been composed at some point after Jesus's death (30s) and, given that Mark was the first Gospel written, before Matthew and Luke constructed their own accounts towards the end of the first century (80–100). While this offers a general period for consideration, the question is whether additional precision can be achieved.

As noted above, scholars generally agree that Mark's emphasis on suffering likely resonates with the community's real-world experience. For this reason, it is helpful to consider possible historical events that may triangulate with the persecution of Mark's community. Scholars often reference two events that may focus the date of composition to a ten-year period from 65 to 75 CE. The first event that possibly influenced Mark's writing and emphasis on suffering was the Neronian persecution. In 64 CE, after a fire broke out in Rome that consumed much of the city, Emperor Nero blamed Christians for the destruction. Although ancient historians suggest that Nero was responsible for the calamity (Suetonius, *Nero* 38; Cassius Dio, *Hist. Rom.* 62.16), Nero persecuted Christians in the most gruesome of ways, burning them on crosses and covering them in animal skins to be mauled by dogs (Tacitus, *Ann.* 15.44). If Mark was written in Rome, as has often been suggested, it is possible that the emphasis on suffering may have been influenced by Nero's persecution of Christians.

The second historical event that may have shaped the narrative was the Jewish war from 66 to 73 CE. The Jewish revolt, which brought significant infighting and violence among Jewish factions, ended with much bloodshed, the devastating fall of Jerusalem, and the burning of the temple at the hands of the Romans. Scholars have long noted that Mark's apocalyptic discourse (ch. 13) contains various elements that may align with these events, including the destruction of the temple (13:2), "wars and rumors of wars" (13:7), and "the desolating sacrilege set up where it ought not to be [that is, in the temple]" (13:14).

Any decision about the historical circumstances that informed the Gospel necessarily has implications for determining the setting of the narrative. Rome seems more probable if the Neronian persecution is the source of the community's suffering. A location near Jerusalem (or Palestine more generally) is plausible if the Jewish war is the primary historical influence. Unfortunately, it is not possible to determine which of these events (or others?) provides the definitive historical backdrop for Mark's Gospel.

Nevertheless, these historical events allow us to more confidently assert a probable time frame for the composition of Mark. Though different interpreters will come to different conclusions about the date of Mark's Gospel (as well as questions of authorship and setting), it is widely affirmed that the second Gospel was composed between 65 and 75 CE and reflects the experience of suffering endured by the Markan community in light of the circumstances surrounding the Neronian persecution or the Jewish war.

(4) STRUCTURE

Subsequent chapters will focus on the interpretation of particular Markan episodes, but it may be helpful to offer a brief overview of the narrative since the arrangement of the material provides a general sense of the author's theological concerns. The challenge, however, in constructing an outline is that it requires the interpreter—even at this early stage—to make judgments about the narrative. Because the author of the Gospel does not provide a structural layout (e.g., a table of contents), any would-be attempt to describe the movement of the narrative is necessarily an interpretive assessment. In this respect, it has often been said that there are as many outlines as there are interpreters. Some outlines are arranged by geography, theology, literary structure, or another overarching, orienting concept. While there is no end to the making of outlines, this is not to suggest that the exercise is without merit. It should simply be observed that such constructs often reveal as much about the interpreter as they do about Mark.

Part of the reason for this conundrum may revolve around assumptions about the text of Mark's Gospel. Mark is a literary document, but it was likely composed to be communicated in an oral medium. This is because the majority of individuals did not have access to Mark's text nor the ability to read extended narratives like Mark's Gospel. It may be helpful to think of Mark as an interwoven tapestry that was written to be performed in an oral arena. Such "texts" are not parceled into neat, divisible sections but are overlapping and linked together by themes and concepts that simultaneously look forward and backward.

Affirming this point does not mean that a structure cannot be discerned in Mark's Gospel, particularly if we focus on the general movements of the narrative. It appears that there are two major parts to Mark's story, which are joined by a middle section that serves as a segue. The first section of the narrative focuses on Jesus's activities in and around Galilee (1:1—8:21). Jesus calls his disciples, performs miracles, and interacts with the religious authorities. Although he amazes crowds and demonstrates authority and power, none of the human characters in the narrative fully understand who he is. The issue of his identity, which surfaces in the opening line of the Gospel (1:1), is a major concern of the narrative but remains elusive to almost everyone except the unclean spirits.

The middle, transitional section of the narrative begins with the healing of a blind man (8:22–26) and continues to focus on the issue of Jesus's identity as he and the disciples make their "way" (8:27; 9:33, 34; 10:17, 32, 46, 52) to Jerusalem. For those who are largely unfamiliar with the story, the scene is strikingly similar to other mighty deeds that Jesus performs. However, as the section progresses it is apparent that the material has been deliberately arranged. The section contains three passion predictions (8:31; 9:30–32; 10:32–34) and is concluded with another restoration of a blind man (10:46–52). The depiction is highly stylized and provides a structural indication that the text has been designed for rhetorical purposes (see ch. 4). As a transitional section the material bridges the two major segments of the Gospel and continues to reflect on the character of Jesus.

The final section likewise seems readily discernible and is centered around the passion (chs. 11–16). The volume of material devoted to the final few days and hours is disproportionate, which is why Mark has often been described as a passion narrative with an extended introduction. The section focuses on the activities in Jerusalem that lead to Jesus's trial, death, and resurrection. The christological significance of these chapters is obvious, even if the depiction of the events and their meaning remains elusive. In particular, both the anticipated reunion with the disciples in Galilee (14:27–28; 16:7) and a formal resurrection appearance are never actualized in the narrative. Mark's story of good news thus terminates on a scene of fear and flight, raising important questions about the nature of Christian discipleship (see ch. 6). Though much more could be said about the literary shape of Mark, the basic structure of the narrative follows three movements:

1. Jesus's ministry of word and deed in and around Galilee (1:1—8:21)

2. Jesus's ministry on the way to Jerusalem (8:22—10:52)

3. Jesus's ministry in Jerusalem, including his trial, death, and resurrection (11:1—16:8)

(5) GENRE

What is genre? Although many people may not be able to offer a definition of the term, they have some understanding of the concept. Most are familiar with movie genres such as comedy, action, drama; or music genres like country, pop, and jazz; or literary genres such as poetry, history, and romance. Generally speaking, the identification of genres allows interpreters to classify and organize particular kinds of artistic expressions. Genre is, as Depew and Obbink suggest, a conceptual orienting device.[1]

But why should interpreters of Mark be concerned about these classification schemes? What difference do they make? Genres are important not only because they help describe categories of artistic expression, but because they create a set of hermeneutical expectations. Genre shapes how an interpreter is to understand a particular artistic work. Thus, if one were to read the following three statements, most interpreters would recognize that we are dealing with three very different genres: 1) Knock-knock . . . 2) According to paragraph c, subsection 1, of article 3b . . . 3) It was a hot summer day in 1965 . . . The identification of these genres (whether consciously or not) frames the interpreter's expectation about whether the statement is a joke, a legal document, or a historical narrative—a distinction that has important interpretive consequences. Unfortunately, many people read the biblical texts without any consideration of genre. They read Mark in the same way they read the Psalms, Paul, and Revelation. The consequence is to conflate genres, which often results in confusion about the meaning of biblical texts.

The question then is what type of genre is Mark? Various theories have been postulated, ranging from folklore to apocalyptic history to novel. More recently a growing number of scholars have concluded that Mark is most similar to Greco-Roman biography. This perspective is, in large part, due to the influential work of Richard Burridge, who has argued that the form, structure, and focus of the text all correspond to features typically found in ancient biography.

1. Depew and Obbink, *Matrices of Genre.*

This does not mean that Mark's Gospel is written in exact correspondence to a Greco-Roman biography but that it displays characteristics typically associated with the genre. All biographies, like all genres, are flexible and malleable. While Mark's genre is closest to a Greco-Roman biography, it nonetheless borrows features from Jewish narratives, apocalyptic thought, and everyday storytelling practices.

This assessment has proven persuasive to many; however, others continue to assert that Mark is not a biography but an entirely new genre. Unlike ancient biographies, Mark's Gospel does not begin with the birth of the main character nor is it focused exclusively with the brief period of history surrounding the central hero (Jesus). Instead, the narrative shows concern for the character of Jesus and the broader activity of God, as well as the ongoing Christian community. Even more telling is that Mark does not identify the text as a biography but rather as a "Gospel" (Mark 1:1). This "Gospel" was taken up by the early church to proclaim the message of Jesus and undoubtedly drew from other genres, such as biography and biblical histories. The Gospel genre was not entirely new but made use of existing genres to communicate Mark's story of Jesus.

While the distinction between these options continues to drive scholarly discussion, what can be affirmed—regardless of genre—is that Mark is a narrative. The second Gospel is a story, a narrative that has been carefully selected and arranged to depict the words and deeds of Jesus. Moreover, Mark makes use of typical storytelling techniques to communicate the Gospel message to the audience (see further discussion in ch. 2).

(6) SOURCES

It seems self-evident that Mark's Gospel makes use of pre-existing traditions about the person and ministry of Jesus. After all, Mark was not an eyewitness and must have received these traditions from somewhere, especially since the second Gospel was the first Gospel written and does not depend on Matthew, Luke, or John. Some of the traditional material used by Mark had likely been formed in the period after the death of Jesus and before the composition of Mark's text. Along these lines, it has often been argued that Mark relies on a pre-Markan version of the passion narrative that described Jesus's final days in Jerusalem, trial, and crucifixion. Other such traditions include the controversy stories in 2:1—3:6 and 11:27—12:37, the parable chapter in 4:1–34, and the apocalyptic discourse in 13:1–37. Still others have argued that Mark's narrative evidences a dependence on Pauline traditions. To be sure, there were traditions about Jesus that circulated after the crucifixion and long before the Gospel of Mark took shape. Mark's reliance on these traditions would not be unusual or surprising given Luke's acknowledgment of a similar practice (Luke 1:1–4).

In view of the fact that Mark likely made use of pre-existing traditions, we may further ask how the author incorporated these traditions into the second Gospel. In the history of scholarship there have been three broad approaches to this question. One view has been to understand Mark as an unsophisticated author whose primary activity was to collect and publish the traditions which had been passed down. For advocates of this approach (i.e., form critics), Mark was an uncreative author who did little more than cut and paste material that had been collected and assembled. Others have suggested that Mark was not an author who was bound to a traditional version of the past, but instead was a creative theologian who wrote from the perspective of his/her own convictions. The by-product of this exercise was a Gospel that unashamedly diverged from tradition in order to present a depiction of Jesus that was dictated by the needs of the community (i.e., redaction critics).

Both of these approaches are attractive in certain respects, but neither is able to account for the array of data in the text itself. An examination of the evidence suggests that Mark was simultaneously concerned about the tradition and a creative theologian. As an illustration of Mark's conservative tendencies, consider the exorcism in Mark 1:21–27. In some respects, the account is similar to other exorcisms in the narrative: Jesus is confronted by an unclean spirit, there is a verbal exchange in which the demon engages Jesus, and the impure spirit is ultimately cast out. What is unusual about 1:21–27 is that the demon identifies Jesus as the "holy one of God" (1:24). This expression is used nowhere else in the second Gospel and, as many have observed, suggests Mark's use of a preexisting tradition. Had the account been composed purely from Mark's imagination, one might have expected the statement to conform to other christological titles that appear more commonly in Mark (i.e., Son of God). Consequently, it could be argued that the use of the designation reflects not only a pre-Markan tradition but the author's fidelity to that tradition.

At the same time, however, there is compelling evidence to suggest that the author was just as comfortable in actively shaping the tradition. That Mark was more than just a conduit is evidenced by the overarching perspective that guided the composition of the text. Starting with the most obvious, it might be observed that Mark has a penchant for certain words and expressions. This is particularly observable in the repeated use of the term "immediately"

(42 times in the narrative) or the grammatical affinity for the historical present (151 times).

Beyond these linguistic examples, there is evidence of Mark's editorial hand at a structural level. It will be shown in subsequent chapters that Mark extends certain themes and has creatively shaped the narrative through the use of rhetorical structures. Though somewhat paradoxical, the analysis suggests that the author of the second Gospel made use of traditions in both a conservative and imaginative fashion.

(7) METHODOLOGY

For beginning students, thinking about the process of interpretation can feel like a conversation of endless abstractions and scholarly nuances. Many wish we could skip this step altogether. Though I am sympathetic to this perspective, two things should be kept in mind. First, everyone has "a method." No one wakes up in the morning with an objective view of the world. We are all shaped by backgrounds and social locations that influence how and what we think, even when we are not consciously aware of it. From gender to race to politics to the place we grew up, each of these dynamics (and more!) guides the way we see and interpret the world around us. This is an inescapable reality of our existence.

Second, no matter how much we might want to dismiss the conversation, method matters. Whether baking cakes or reading the Bible, the product that is produced is often determined by the methods we use. Each of us is guided by assumptions (i.e., methods) that influence our perception of the world. This is true regardless of whether we can articulate or justify a particular methodological approach. Having an awareness of these methods has the potential of exposing our biases as well as revealing questions and possibilities for consideration.

Of course, this is not a book about interpretive methods, so I offer only a few brief comments in order to clarify the perspective guiding my own discussion of this journey. Biblical studies is a world governed by diverse methodological approaches. Some of the interpretive methods are new, some are old, some are historical, some are sociological, and some are this, that, and the other. The methodological diversity is now an inherent part of the conversation, even if it has been received in different ways. Some lament the myriad of approaches and the fragmentation it has produced. Others, like myself, are inclined to view the complexity and variation as a strength, not a weakness. New approaches come with new questions that have the potential of illuminating ancient texts and revealing new angles of vision.

However, given the introductory nature of this book, there will be no attempt to produce an exhaustive analysis of the text from every methodological angle, if such a thing were possible. The discussion will instead incorporate insights gleaned from narrative and performance criticisms. Put simply, the methodological focus will be to understand Mark's story as a narrative with a nod towards the reception of the text in performance. Priority will be given to understanding Mark's Gospel as a coherent and creative story—without neglecting the first-century historical context—while also recognizing that the text was likely performed in an oral context.

There are a variety of reasons for this approach, though my primary concern is to help students appreciate the distinct contributions of the second evangelist. All too often students have a somewhat blurred understanding of the Gospels, as though they each tell the same story about

Jesus. When the texts do diverge, the impulse is to harmonize the accounts. Though there may well be a place for this type of reading, it is important to recognize that there are four Gospels, not one. Each of these texts can and should be appreciated on its own terms, recognizing of course that no one text exists in a historical, political, or sociological vacuum. The concern of this volume is to explore the portrait of Jesus in the Gospel of Mark in order to understand Mark's unique contribution to the NT.

CONCLUSION

Having addressed several of the background issues that are foundational to the study of Mark, the remainder of the volume will focus on the text of Mark's Gospel. Chapter 2 will explore some of the techniques and structures utilized by Mark to tell the story of Jesus. Chapter 3 will look specifically at the depiction of Jesus and the various points of emphasis that are accentuated in Mark's narrative. Chapter 4 will examine the disciples and the strikingly harsh depiction of the Twelve. Chapter 5 will consider the so-called messianic secret, another widely recognized and important theme in Mark. Finally, chapter 6 will conclude by wrestling with Mark's abrupt and truncated ending, seeking to understand why the narrative concludes in a such a strange fashion. No doubt, there are other interesting questions and issues raised by Mark's Gospel, but it is hoped that this selection of material will offer beginning students an entry point into the fascinating world of Markan studies.

FURTHER READING

Beavis, Mary Ann. *Mark*. Paideia. Grand Rapids: Baker, 2011.
Boring, M. Eugene. *Mark: A Commentary*. NTL. Louisville: Westminster John Knox, 2006.

Collins, Adela Yarbro. *Mark: A Commentary*. Hermeneia. Minneapolis: Fortress, 2007.

Focant, Camille. *The Gospel according to Mark: A Commentary*. Translated by Leslie Robert Keylock. Eugene, OR: Pickwick Publciations, 2012.

France, R. T. *The Gospel of Mark: A Commentary on the Greek Text*. NIGTC. Grand Rapids: Eerdmans, 2002.

Marcus, Joel. *Mark 1–8: A New Translation with Introduction and Commentary*. AB 27. New York: Doubleday, 2000.

———. *Mark 8–16: A New Translation with Introduction and Commentary*. AB 27A. New Haven: Yale University Press, 2009.

Moloney, Francis J. *The Gospel of Mark: A Commentary*. Peabody, MA: Hendrickson, 2002.

2

NARRATIVE DYNAMICS IN MARK

ONE OF THE CHALLENGES for beginning students is appreciating the narrative dynamics of the Gospels. Most recognize that the Gospels include various episodes depicting the teaching and ministry of Jesus. But many have not considered how the arrangement of episodes shapes the interpretive process. Such an impulse comes naturally as sermons, books, and devotional materials frequently model this practice. The implicit assumption seems to be that individual episodes can be interpreted in relative isolation. While this approach may be well intended, it misunderstands the narrative dynamics of the Gospels.

To illustrate the importance of context, I often show students a picture from the book *Pooh's Best Day*.[1] In the scene, Pooh, Tiger, Christopher Robin, and Piglet are inside a house. Numerous jars of honey have been placed around

---

1. Disney, *Pooh's Best Day*.

the room as a smiling Pooh clutches a green, open container with honey dripping down the sides. Together the four friends build a makeshift tent using a sheet, a coat rack, a box, and a chair. In the corner of the room, a window reveals the rain and lightning outside as the activities unfold.

Once students have had sufficient opportunity to observe the scene, I inquire why Pooh and company are building a tent inside the house. Responses typically focus on the idea that the characters are at play or that the inclement weather necessitates that the group stay inside. After student reflections have been exhausted, I offer my interpretation. I suggest that Pooh is deeply troubled and has experienced a falling out with the Pooh community over matters of theological importance. The tent is designed to isolate and shield Pooh (and his friends) from adversaries in the community. Though he appears happy, the wry smile hides his emotional pain and feelings of rejection. He clings to the jar of honey as it remains one of the few things that brings him joy and contentment. Despite all appearances, Pooh is deeply discouraged and needs to be restored to his community.

Following my description, I ask students to assess my interpretation. Some students sit in quiet amazement, stunned by my interpretive prowess. Others, in respectful and kind ways, encourage me to seek professional help. Most of my students simply shake their heads in disbelief. It is evident, of course, that my perspective is unpopular, but I push students to articulate *why* they disagree. They are often unsure how to express their disagreement, much less to evaluate the perspectives.

At this point, I read the entirety of *Pooh's Best Day* and ask students to reconsider their responses. Collectively, we come to two conclusions. First, Pooh has not been rejected by his community but is enjoying a day with friends. Pooh's best day is a day with friends (and honey too) regardless of the atmospheric conditions. The second conclusion has broader implications and is the point of the exercise. Whether considering a book, a movie, or the Gospel of Mark, the narrative guides the interpretation of the individual parts. Indeed, without a context it is difficult, if not impossible, to dismiss an interpretation. Though some texts may be open to more than one perspective, to neglect the context opens the door for confusion and distortion.

The aim of this chapter is to help students appreciate the patterns, techniques, and structures that undergird Mark's Gospel and thereby create the interpretive context to understand the narrative. Though students often acknowledge the importance of context, many are not familiar with the ways in which Mark's narrative is structured. These techniques are woven into the fabric of the Gospel and are designed to inform the interpretive task. Though the story is often linked by thematic content, it also uses patterns and structural devices to connect episodes that may appear unrelated. These devices often signal the interpretive context by which a particular episode should be appreciated. In this respect, it is important to consider not only *what* is communicated but *how* it is communicated. The remainder of the chapter will explore several features and/or structures that are used to tell Mark's story of good news.

(1) VERBAL REPETITION

One of the more obvious storytelling techniques in Mark's Gospel is the use of verbal repetition. Verbal repetition involves the repeated use of particular words and/or phrases. Often this occurs within a single episode. For example, in Mark 11:27–33 the term "authority" is used four times in seven verses (11:28[2x], 29, 33). In such instances the repeated word or phrase is a not-so-subtle clue that a concept or theme is a focal point of the narrative.

Consider the repeated use of the term "king" in Mark 15. The word occurs six times in the trial and crucifixion scene (15:2, 9, 12, 18, 26, 32). Yet up until this point, Mark has refrained from describing Jesus as a "king." Why? The passion affirms that Jesus is a king, albeit a different kind than what many likely expected. Jesus is not a king who lords his power over others (cf. 10:43–45); rather his kingship is defined by humility and service as exemplified by his death on the cross. The use of this kind of repetition is a frequent occurrence in Mark and accentuates particular ideas and concepts.

Just as repetition occurs within episodes, it also occurs between episodes. In such instances, the repeated use of a term and/or phrase may be used to link episodes across the narrative. For example, scholars have long observed that Mark's Gospel contains two feeding accounts (6:31–44; 8:1–9). The episodes are not adjacent to one another, but there is nonetheless a striking level of correspondence. In each instance, Jesus "takes" (6:41; 8:6) "bread" (6:37, 38, 41[2x], 44; 8:4, 5, 6) and "fish" (6:38, 41[2x], 43; 8:7), offers a "blessing" (6:41; 8:7), and has the items distributed to the "crowd" (6:34; 8:1, 2, 6[2x]).

In both contexts, the crowds "eat" (6:42; 8:8) and are "satisfied" (6:42; 8:8). At first glance, the similarity of terms may seem unsurprising since the episodes are similar in nature. However, it is often argued that the language is intentional and is designed to draw attention and comparison between the two scenes. One notable difference between the accounts is that the first feeding takes place in Jewish territory, while the second takes place in gentile territory. More will be said about these passages in subsequent chapters, but for now it is sufficient to observe that the similarities underscore God's blessings for all people—both Jews and gentiles.

Verbal repetition, both within and between episodes, is a frequent occurrence in narrative; however, it would be inaccurate to suggest that this is the only type of repetition. Mark often exhibits a kind of near repetition. In such instances, the narrative utilizes different terms that are synonymous or close in meaning. This kind of repetition represents a roundabout way of effectively achieving the same result, while preserving some verbal variation.

Consider the scene in Mark 6:45–52 and 53–56. In the first episode, Jesus sends the disciples ahead of him to cross the sea, while he stays behind to pray. During the night as the disciples struggle to make headway against the wind, Jesus comes down from a mountain and begins to walk on water. As Jesus is about to pass by, the disciples "see" (6:49) Jesus and become frightened, thinking he is a ghost. After Jesus enters the boat and the winds cease, the boat comes to shore. The narrative then shifts to what appears to be a quick summary of Jesus's ministerial activities in and around Gennesaret, the place where Jesus and the disciples eventually disembark from the boat (6:53–56). As soon as Jesus gets out of the boat, Mark indicates that the people "recognized" (6:54) Jesus. Of note are the two terms in v. 49 and v. 54 ("see" and "recognize"). Though the words have slightly different shades of meaning, there is semantic overlap for what appears to be an intentional point of comparison. The accounts have been stylized in order to draw a link between the two scenes. Although the disciples have been made insiders to the teachings and works of Jesus, they do not identify him walking on the water—performing a deed that only he has demonstrated the ability to accomplish thus far in the narrative. Ironically, it is not the disciples who recognize Jesus, but *outsiders* living in the villages and towns around Gennesaret. The similar terminology provides an interpretive echo that facilitates drawing a connection between events. As is often the case with repetition, this simple technique is a rhetorical device used for the benefit of the audience.

(2) SANDWICH

Perhaps the most distinctive storytelling technique associated with Mark's Gospel is a sandwich. Yes, a sandwich. This storytelling device, also referred to as intercalation, involves two episodes that are structured like a sandwich. The first episode forms the outer portion of the sandwich (the bread) and is divided into two segments. The sandwich begins with the first episode but is interrupted or left unresolved. The second episode follows immediately thereafter and functions as the middle portion of the sandwich (the meat). The narrative then returns to the first scene to conclude the intercalated sequence. Generally speaking, the two episodes are readily distinguishable and typically involve different characters and/or circumstances in the constituent elements of the sandwich.

A classic example of this technique is found in Mark 5:21–43. The two episodes both involve stories of healing. In the first (5:21–24), Jesus is confronted by Jairus, a synagogue leader whose daughter is sick and near the point of death. As Jesus makes his way to the man's house, the story is interrupted. The middle portion of the sandwich narrates the account of the hemorrhaging woman (5:25–34). The scene describes an unnamed woman who has had a flow of blood for twelve years (5:25) and has suffered under many doctors. When the woman hears of Jesus's presence, she sneaks up, touches his cloak, and is immediately healed (5:29). After the woman comes forward, Jesus declares that her faith has healed her. The narrative then returns to the story of Jairus (5:35–43), which began in vv. 21–24. As the story of the hemorrhaging woman concludes, news comes that Jairus's daughter has passed. Despite what appears to be a futile situation, Jesus returns to Jairus's home. Taking the girl by the hand, Jesus commands her to "get up" (5:41). The girl, who Mark mentions is twelve years old (5:42), rises immediately and begins to walk.

Markan Sandwich

Story 1------Jairus approaches Jesus (5:21–24)
  Story 2---Hemorrhaging woman is healed (5:25–34)
Story 1------Jesus heals Jairus's daughter (5:35–43)

Given the frequency of Markan sandwiches (e.g., 3:20–35; 6:7–30; 11:12–21; 14:1–11; 14:53–72), it is reasonable to consider the function of these narrative devices. Students sometimes suggest that the structure mirrors the historical circumstances and that the evangelist is merely recording what transpired in real life. This may be a possibility, but it may not tell the full story. First, even if the events did occur in this order, it is imperative to remember that Mark has selected *which events to include in the narrative.* Second, as a creative interpreter Mark has also selected *how to arrange the material in the narrative.* To this point, it is interesting to observe that some of the stories that Mark has intercalated are de-sandwiched by Matthew and Luke (e.g., Mark 11:12–21//Matt 21:12–22//Luke 19:45–48)— both of whom write after Mark and use the second Gospel as a source text. Thus, later Gospel writers did not think it necessary to narrate certain events in Mark using the same structure type.

If the sequencing of material is not dictated by a concern for historical remembrance, then why are the episodes structured in this fashion? Many have argued that the arrangement of material serves a rhetorical and theological purpose. The juxtaposition of scenes invites the audience to consider the relationship between the two episodes—to reflect on a particular theme or idea that is given texture and nuance by the intercalation. Take the sequence of events in Mark 5:21–43. The narrator seems to invite a comparison both by the structure and by the verbal repetition between scenes. The seemingly extraneous detail relating the time period in which the woman has suffered (twelve years [5:25]) and the age of the young girl (twelve years old [5:42]) are subtle cues that link the two "daughters" (5:34–35). The explicit connection invites further reflection and appreciation. The interspersing of these scenes deepens central themes of the narrative (e.g., faith and discipleship) and has "unwritten implications," which are "unformulated in the text" yet represent its intention.[2]

Recognizing the structure is therefore more than a passing literary interest but has theological ramifications for understanding Mark's Gospel.

(3) FRAME

Another technique found in Mark's Gospel is the use of framing episodes. Framing occurs when two similar episodes bracket a segment of the narrative. The relationship between episodes is often based on thematic concerns, and the two episodes may encompass either small or large portions of the narrative. Students sometimes confuse frames and sandwiches since both structure types bracket a portion of text. However, there is a twofold distinction. First, a sandwich begins with a single episode that is broken into two parts, whereas a frame utilizes two distinct episodes

2. Iser, "Reading Process," 281, 292.

that are thematically related. Second, a frame brackets a segment that spans beyond a single episode, whereas the inner portion of a sandwich is made up of a single episode.

As has already been discussed in the previous chapter, one of the often-cited examples of framing occurs in relation to the two healing episodes in the middle portion of Mark's Gospel. Both episodes revolve around the restoration of sight (8:22–26; 10:45–52) and the two scenes frame the various interactions and passion predictions that transpire as Jesus is on his way to Jerusalem. Another example of this technique occurs in relation to the eschatological discourse in Mark 13. Scholars have long noted that the extended discourse is framed by stories of two anonymous women, the poor widow in the temple (12:41–44) and the woman who anoints Jesus for burial (14:3–9). Perhaps the most extensive frame occurs at the beginning and end of Mark's Gospel and is christological in nature. As Jesus is baptized, the heavens are torn open and a voice from heaven declares Jesus to be the beloved Son (1:9–11). A similar event transpires at the end of the Gospel; however, this time it is at the crucifixion of Jesus. Immediately after Jesus dies, the veil of the temple is torn from top to bottom and the centurion overseeing the events declares that Jesus is the Son of God (15:37–39). Although the scenes appear unrelated, both make use of the same Greek term to describe a "tearing" (1:10; 15:38) in the narrative.

Several of these examples will be discussed in further detail in the subsequent chapters but a few summative comments are in order. First, the use of frames (as with the other structure types) adds an organizational component that calls attention to the intentionality of Mark's literary design. The aesthetic symmetry signals to the interpreter that the episodes are more than a random collection of stories. Second, the deliberate structuring invites reflection on the sequencing of events and their literary relationship. Though frames may not be as robustly connected as intercalated episodes, the structure typically points interpreters to one of the central concerns of the Gospel.

(4) CHIASM

Mark sometimes employs a technique that may seem foreign to modern interpreters, but in actuality is well attested in the ancient world. This structuring device, known as a chiasm (based on the shape of the Greek letter chi, χ), involves multiple, thematically related episodes that are arranged in a concentric pattern. The structure follows an A B C B' A' pattern, whereby the outer (A, A') and inner (B, B') episodes share some point of commonality. The central episode in the unit functions as a pivot point and often serves as an interpretive key for the entire structural device.

Mark 2:1—3:6 is an often-cited passage involving this organizing principle. There are five discernible episodes in the unit, each of which involves some sort of conflict between Jesus and the religious leaders. While these controversies provide a rationale for the arrangement, a closer look reveals additional points of similarity and differentiation. The outer episodes (A, A') begin with a similar phrase ("And again he entered" [2:1; 3:1]) and involve physical healings that raise questions about the law. The inner episodes (B, B'), in contrast, deal with the issue of eating and likewise prompt questions about Jesus's actions. Episodes A and B are linked together by the catchword "sins" (2:9) or "sinners" (3:16 [2x]), just as B' and A' are linked by the term "Sabbath" (2:23, 24, 27 [2x], 28; 3:2, 3). The central section on fasting (C) acts as a pivot point around which the entire unit is structured. Collectively, the sequence of events is arranged in a typical chiastic pattern.

Chiasm

A Healing of the Paralytic (2:1–12)
  B Eating with Tax Collectors and Sinners (2:13–17)
    C Fasting (2:18–22)
  B' Eating on the Sabbath (2:23–28)
A' Healing the Man with the Withered Hand (3:1–6)

The arrangement is evidence of Mark's editorial skill, but there is more than creative design behind the structure. At the center of the chiasm Jesus reveals that "the days will come when the bridegroom is taken away from them, and then they will fast on that day" (2:20). While the reference to fasting fits nicely with the emphasis on eating in B and B', this is the first reference to Jesus's impending death, albeit as an allusion. Moreover, that Jesus is to be "taken away" (2:20) must be interpreted against the series of controversies surrounding the religious leaders. In other words, the chiastic arrangement, coupled with Jesus's statement in 2:20, foreshadows the remainder of the story. Additional details will follow, but there is a growing and ominous sense in which Jesus's conflict with the religious leaders will take a fateful turn. To this end, the final verse in the chiasm points in this direction as the religious leaders begin to plot how they might "destroy him [Jesus]" (3:6).

These types of patterns may be challenging for modern readers. But ancient audiences were attuned to the practices and would have readily discerned these types of structural relationships. With a bit of practice and an eye towards understanding, modern readers can develop the same ability to identify chiastic relationships.

(5) PATTERNS OF THREE

Like many narratives, both ancient and modern, Mark's Gospel displays a penchant for threes. This stylistic device involves a form of repetition that may be used independently or in conjunction with one of the other structure types. Groupings of three are fairly generous and may involve people, events, or situations. The elements may function within episodes or between episodes and may be chronologically separated from one another.

Sometimes these groupings involve elements within the narrative that are described in the form of a list. For example, in Mark 3:35, Jesus indicates that whoever does the will of God is his brother, sister, and mother. In 4:8, during the parable of the soils, Jesus describes the good seed as producing a crop, some of which multiplied thirty, sixty, or a hundred times. Likewise, in 11:27, as Jesus enters Jerusalem, he is confronted by the chief priests, scribes, and elders. In each instance, the narrative provides an explicit series of three that further underscores the narrator's affinity for the pattern.

On other occasions, the three elements have a structural emphasis. In Gethsemane, for example, Jesus instructs Peter, James, and John (three disciples) to keep watch while he goes off to pray. He returns three separate times but only to find the three disciples sleeping (14:32–41). The depiction of Peter's denial also exemplifies this type of tripartite progression (14:66–72). The scene is constructed around three interactions between Peter and those standing near him in the courtyard of the high priest (14:66–68, 69–70a, 70b–72). Or consider the Roman trial, where Pilate questions the crowd three times (15:9, 12, 14). And at the crucifixion, Mark structures the account around three-hour intervals (15:25, 33a, 33b).

In still other uses, the threefold pattern occurs in a combination of episodes. Thus, there are three calls or commissioning scenes involving the disciples (1:16–20; 3:13–19; 6:7–13). There are three passion predictions in which Jesus instructs the disciples about his impending death and resurrection (8:31; 9:31; 10:32–34). And there are three boat scenes in which there is some form of conflict between Jesus and the disciples as they make their way across the sea (4:34–41; 6:45–53; 8:13–21).

The weight of evidence suggests that Mark displays a penchant for threes. Some of these examples (particularly the lists) may indicate nothing more than an effective and aesthetically pleasing storytelling technique that Mark has imbibed from his cultural surroundings. Other examples, however, have a more discernible interpretive significance in order to emphasize the third and climactic event in the triad. In this respect, Peter's final denial is the most emphatic (14:70b–72), just as the third passion prediction is the most explicit (10:32–34). The prevalence of the structure across the narrative leads the interpreter to anticipate the technique, thereby creating suspense and intrigue as the pattern unfolds.

(6) QUESTIONS

Mark's Gospel contains a number of questions. In fact, among the Synoptics, Mark has the highest proportion of questions—sometimes stacking questions on top of one another (e.g., 4:21, 40; 6:3; 8:17; 9:19; 11:28; 12:14; 14:37). In total, there are 111 questions in the relatively short sixteen chapters of Mark's Gospel. Except for God, each of the main character groups poses questions, including Jesus, the disciples, the religious leaders, the supplicants of the narrative—even the demons.

Perhaps it is not surprising that we find so many questions in Mark's Gospel since questions are a necessary and natural part of human interaction. "How many loaves do you have?" (6:38); "What are you arguing about with them?" (9:16); "What are you doing, untying the colt?" (11:5); "Why do you trouble her?" (14:6). One might conclude that there is nothing significant about these questions since they simply move the plot along. This, of course, is true. But it is also important to observe that questions often have more than an informational purpose. That is, they are not only a vehicle by which information is exchanged between characters. Questions are a communication tool used by the characters, but many of the questions appear to have a rhetorical purpose that invites active participation by the interpreter.

Take the following example. Throughout the first half of the narrative, there is a strong focus on the identity of Jesus. Jesus performs miracles and demonstrates authority, but no one—except the unclean spirits and God—knows who Jesus is. In 4:35, Jesus enters into a boat with the disciples to cross to the other side of the sea. As the group sets out, a fierce storm arises that threatens to sink the boat. Although several of the disciples are professional fisherman, there is tremendous panic and fear. Eventually, the disciples wake Jesus who is sleeping in the stern of the boat. With a simple word, Jesus rebukes the wind and sea and brings immediate calm to the chaotic moment. Jesus then rebukes the disciples with a series of questions (4:40), which prompts the disciples to pose a question of their own: "Who is this that even the wind and sea obey him?" (4:41). What is interesting is that the question is not answered by Jesus or the disciples. The question is left dangling at the end of the scene as if to tantalize the interpreter. *Who is this Jesus?* There will be numerous clues as the story progresses, but for now the explicit, unanswered question is left for the audience to ponder.

One gets the impression that, in fact, many of the questions in Mark are ultimately intended for the interpreter. "Do you not yet understand" (8:17); "Who do you say that I am?" (8:29); "For what will it profit . . . [a person] to gain the whole world and forfeit their life?" (8:36); "What must I do to inherit eternal life?" (10:17). Although each of these questions serves a purpose in its narrative setting, as the interpreter overhears the various exchanges, they are pulled into the drama and confronted with the same questions addressed to the characters. Such rhetorical moves are subtle, but they are no less effective. Mark's use of questions is just one indication that the narrative is written for and with the interpreter in mind.

Questions occur so frequently in life and narrative that we may not have considered how they function in a text like Mark. Beyond the purpose they serve between characters, it is important to consider how they contribute to the overall effect of the narrative. The use of questions in the second Gospel frequently invites interpreters to become a participant in the drama. More importantly, they subtly encourage the audience to consider what Mark assumes are crucial questions for all would-be followers of Jesus.

CONCLUSION

Mark's Gospel is not a random collection of sayings or episodes about Jesus. It is not a patchwork of traditions that the author has uncritically stitched together. It is not simply a moment-by-moment account of what happened in the life of the historical Jesus. This, of course, is not to dismiss the historical or to suggest that Mark did not borrow from well-established traditions. It is to say that the second

Gospel is *more* than just a historical account or collection of traditions. Mark's Gospel displays a creative and deliberate arrangement of material. The various structures of the Gospel suggest that the text is a carefully arranged, purposeful articulation of the Jesus narrative.

The discussion of narrative patterns may seem uninspiring. After all, most reading this book are not necessarily interested in the finer details of literary structures. But appreciating Mark requires an understanding of how the Gospel is constructed. Because form and content are woven together, the two are inextricably bound in the narrative. Understanding how the narrative is assembled—the literary structures—helps one to discern what the author is communicating. Although the Gospels are often treated like Humpty Dumpty, shattered and broken into bits and pieces, the arrangement of Mark suggests that the author intended the Gospel to be appreciated as a literary whole. In the discussions that follow, the goal is to understand several of the central issues in Mark through this wholistic, narrative perspective.

QUESTIONS FOR REFLECTION

1. Identify three narrative techniques utilized in Mark. What are the distinguishing characteristics of these devices?

2. In what ways are narrative structures and patterns an interpretive aid?

FURTHER READING

Brown, Jeannine K. *Gospels as Stories: A Narrative Approach to Matthew, Mark, Luke, and John*. Grand Rapids: Baker, 2020.

Edwards, James R. "Markan Sandwiches: The Significance of Interpolations in Markan Narratives." *NovT* (1989) 193–216.

Malbon, Elizabeth Struthers. *Hearing Mark: A Listener's Guide.* Harrisburg, PA: Trinity, 2002.

Resseguie, James L. *Narrative Criticism of the New Testament: An Introduction.* Grand Rapids: Baker, 2005.

Rhoads, David, et al. *Mark as Story: An Introduction to the Narrative of a Gospel.* 3rd ed. Minneapolis: Fortress, 2012.

3

"WHO DO YOU SAY THAT I AM?"

Mark's Jesus

It comes as no surprise that Jesus is the central figure of Mark's Gospel. From beginning to end, his interactions, deeds, and teachings dominate the narrative. But who is the Markan Jesus? And how is the character of Jesus portrayed in the second Gospel?

Any understanding of Mark's Jesus must take account of the narrative. This requires appreciating what Jesus does, what he says, as well as how other characters interact with him. Though this observation may seem self-evident, many students have preconceived ideas about Jesus that cloud their understanding of the narrative. These assumptions are derived from various sources and are often unwittingly projected onto the text. While these notions may cohere with certain church or Gospel traditions, Mark's Jesus must be understood on Mark's terms. That is, in order to understand the portrayal of Jesus in the second Gospel—Mark's Christology—priority must be given to the text itself. The following discussion will therefore lay particular emphasis on the narrative depiction of Jesus in Mark's Gospel.

It goes without saying that a detailed account of Mark's Jesus is beyond the scope of this chapter. The more modest objective is to introduce students to a discussion of Mark's Christology. To this end, the focus will be clustered around three concerns: 1) the characterization of Jesus, 2) the relationship between Jesus and God, and 3) the purpose of Jesus's death.

DEFINING CHARACTER TRAITS

Mark's Jesus is a character in the narrative. This is not to deny that Jesus was a real historical figure. It is to affirm that the presentation of Jesus comes to us by way of a literary portrait. The character of Jesus is embedded in a narrative and ascribed traits and characteristics. Although there are numerous aspects of this characterization that might be explored, the following will consider Jesus's authority and power, his compassion for gentiles, and his service and suffering. These characteristics are widely affirmed and will help situate the broader discussion of Mark's Christology before moving on to more disputed matters in the latter portion of the chapter.

Authority and Power

One of the defining characteristics of Mark's Jesus is his authority and power. Having been affirmed by God (1:11) and empowered by the Spirit (1:10), his first expression of authority comes with the command to repent and believe (1:15). The manifestation of this authority is displayed in the very next scene when Jesus calls the first disciples (1:16–20). Thereafter, Jesus and the disciples enter a synagogue in Capernaum where Jesus begins to teach and heal. Though the content of Jesus's teaching is not mentioned, the people respond in amazement to the demonstration of his power, noting his "authority" (1:22, 27) vis-à-vis the teachers of the law (1:22). Though brief, the opening episodes lay the groundwork for an important theme that will be developed throughout the narrative, a few illustrations of which are noted below.

One of the more notable examples of Jesus's authority and power occurs in 4:35—5:43. At first glance, the four episodes appear to be a random collection of miracles. Upon careful inspection, however, the sequence displays a well-crafted arrangement that accentuates Jesus's dominion over the created order. The section begins with Jesus and the disciples as they cross the sea of Galilee (4:35–41). A fierce storm develops that threatens the integrity of the boat (4:37). Much to the disciples' dismay, Jesus is asleep in the stern of the boat seemingly oblivious to the situation (4:38–39). After he is aroused, Jesus pronounces an authoritative word that quiets the wind and sea (4:39). Although the storm causes the disciples to be concerned for their lives, the display of Jesus's power ironically prompts the Twelve to "fear a great fear" (4:41).

The narrative then transitions to the second miracle (5:1–20), where once again Jesus and the disciples enter a boat to cross the sea of Galilee (5:1). Upon landfall, Jesus is approached by a man with an unclean spirit. In perhaps the most detailed exorcism in the entire Gospel tradition, Mark describes the dire situation of a man possessed by a "legion" of demons (5:2–9). After a brief exchange in which the demonic host identifies Jesus as the "Son of the Most High God" (5:7), the demons enter a nearby herd of swine that subsequently rush headlong into the sea (5:12–13). When the townspeople are informed of these events, they become afraid and plead with Jesus to leave the region (5:14–17).

The third and fourth miracles are sandwiched together (see ch. 2), indicating a deliberate literary strategy that is often freighted with theological implications. Though the juxtaposition of these scenes is intriguing, the concern here is the macrostructure and how the third and fourth miracles function within the larger unit. The events of 5:21–43 begin with Jesus and the disciples having again crossed the sea of Galilee (5:21). As Jesus is surrounded by a large crowd, a synagogue official named Jairus approaches, falls at Jesus's feet, and begs him to heal his ailing daughter (5:21–24).

Jesus begins to depart with Jairus when the scene is interrupted by the story of the hemorrhaging woman (5:25–34). An unnamed woman who has suffered from a flow of blood for twelve years (5:25) approaches Jesus and touches his garment (5:27). The woman is immediately healed, and Jesus recognizes that power has departed from him. In the quest to determine what has taken place, the woman approaches Jesus and, like Jairus, falls at his feet (5:33; cf. 5:22). The woman acknowledges her actions and is commended for her faith before being sent away (5:34).

As the story of the hemorrhaging woman concludes, the scene shifts quickly back to the Jairus narrative (5:35–43). Representatives from Jairus's house bring news that his little girl has died. Jesus instructs Jairus to "believe" (5:36) and proceeds to the house where they find weeping and wailing (5:38–39). Taking only the father and mother, along with Peter, James, and John, Jesus enters into the house and commands the girl to "get up" (5:41). Like the hemorrhaging woman, the girl is immediately restored and begins to walk around (5:42).

Taken together these four miracles showcase the power and authority of Jesus. Each individually attests to the unique ministry of Jesus as he effectively navigates dire situations. In the first episode (4:35–41), Jesus demonstrates authority over the forces of wind and sea; in the second, he takes on a legion of demons and exorcises them from a possessed man (5:1–20); in the third and fourth accounts, Jesus heals a woman with a prolonged medical issue (5:25–34) and raises a girl from the dead (5:21–24, 35–43). These four scenes represent powerful expressions of healing and restoration. But they also communicate beyond the sum of the individual parts. The deliberate structuring hints that there is no earthly or supernatural force, including nature, demons, disease, or even death itself, that is able to subvert the "power" of Jesus (5:30). As God's eschatological agent, Jesus possesses authority over the totality of the created order.

While it is natural to gravitate to the mighty deeds in order to appreciate Jesus's authority and power, the narrative also expresses these characteristics in other ways. For example, as Jesus and the disciples are passing through a grainfield on the day of the Sabbath, the disciples begin to pick heads of grain (2:23–28). The Pharisees—perceiving this to be a violation of the Sabbath—question Jesus about the disciples' actions. The Markan Jesus responds by pointing to the story of David who entered the house of God to eat from the consecrated bread (2:25–26). Along with this scriptural precedent, Jesus underscores his interpretive authority by noting that "the Son of Man is lord even of the sabbath" (2:28). Similar encounters occur throughout the narrative as Jesus is questioned about matters of religious importance (2:18–22; 3:1–6; 7:1–13; 10:2–12; 12:13–17, 18–27, 28–34). Though the leaders often seek to test Jesus (and thereby undermine his reputation among the crowds), they are invariably silenced and become foils who highlight Jesus's authoritative interpretation of the Jewish Scriptures.

Along with his mighty deeds and understanding of Scripture, Jesus's authority is also revealed in his prophetic pronouncements. On various occasions, Jesus speaks about future events. Some of these predictions describe matters beyond the story (e.g., Mark 13; 14:27–28), while others are fulfilled within the plotted narrative. The latter occur with some frequency in Mark's story. For instance, Jesus accurately describes 1) where the disciples will find a colt needed for his entrance into the city (11:2–4); 2) a meeting with a man carrying a water jar who is to provide accommodation for the Passover (14:13–16); 3) his betrayal by one of the disciples (14:18, 43–46); and 4) Peter's threefold denial (14:30, 66–72). Even after Jesus is arrested, the narrative continues to unfold according to his authoritative word. While he is blindfolded, punched, and spit on, he is mockingly instructed to "prophesy" (14:65). What the soldiers do not realize is that at the moment of this utterance, two of Jesus's prophecies are being fulfilled: 1) Peter is outside denying Jesus for the third time (14:66–72), and 2) the arrest signals the realization of his threefold passion prediction (8:31; 9:31; 10:32–34). These examples underscore that Jesus is imbued with prophetic insight and that his word "will not pass away" (13:31).

In all of these expressions, the character of Jesus displays power and authority. Whether it be invoked in the healing of an unclean supplicant, the correct understanding of the law, or a prediction about future events, Jesus displays a God-given authority to whom the characters in the narrative are instructed to "listen" (9:7). There are, however, a few instances where Jesus's authority appears to be limited or restrained. On two occasions Jesus explicitly commands a supplicant and/or group of individuals to refrain from speaking about his mighty deeds (1:44–45; 7:36). In both situations, the individual(s) disobey. A similar limitation is suggested when Jesus affirms that he does not have authority to grant who may sit at his right or left hand (10:40). How the interpreter is to understand these variations will be discussed below, but it seems relatively certain that the manifestation of Jesus's authority is a central concern of the narrative. To a certain extent, it is the response to Jesus's power and authority that drives the plot forward.

Compassion for Gentiles

Mark's Jesus is a Jewish man who comes in fulfillment of Jewish Scriptures for the Jewish people. But in no way is Jesus's ministry exclusive to the Jewish people. Mark's Jesus takes three journeys into gentile territory and inaugurates a gentile mission (5:1–20; 7:24—8:10; 8:22—9:29). The attention devoted to these journeys underscores the gentile response, as well as God's love and compassion for all people. The theme of inclusion is woven into the fabric of the narrative and is a hallmark of Mark's christological portrait.

The gentile mission does not begin until 5:1–20, but three factors foreshadow Jesus's ministry beyond Israel's borders. First, Jesus receives gentiles in the Jewish homeland at the outset of his ministry. As news of his deeds spreads in and beyond the Jewish homeland, Mark indicates that Jesus withdrew to the sea, followed by a multitude of people (3:7–8). Among the crowds are individuals from Galilee, Judea, Jerusalem, as well as Idumea, beyond the Jordan, and the vicinity of Tyre and Sidon. These latter three regions, to the north (Tyre and Sidon), south (Idumea), and east (beyond the Jordan), represent gentile territories outside the Jewish homeland. In this first encounter with gentiles, Jesus makes no attempt to avoid foreigners nor does he differentiate based on ethnicity (3:10–11). He willingly heals Jews and gentiles and thus foreshadows his own mission to gentiles later in the narrative.

Second, Jesus's eventual crossing of geographic boundaries is preceded by the crossing of religious boundaries. On various occasions, the Markan Jesus disregards and/or reinterprets religious traditions espoused by the Jewish establishment. He touches a leper (1:41), dines with sinners and tax collectors (2:15–17), lays aside religious practices (2:18–22), and repeatedly transgresses the Sabbath (2:23–28; 3:1–6). The Markan Jesus is not constrained by the expectations of his contemporaries as new wine calls for new wineskins (2:22). These episodic boundary crossings, while they do not point exclusively to a gentile mission, pave the way for the transgression of additional boundaries as the narrative progresses.

Third, Jesus's teaching anticipates the expansion of the kingdom and the mission to the gentiles. The audience learns in Mark's parables chapter that God's kingdom is not to be hidden but is to illuminate and bring revelation (4:21–23). Though it begins small like a mustard seed (4:30), it grows apart from human intervention (4:26–27) and ultimately produces "large branches, so that the birds of the air can make nests in its shade" (4:32). This reference to birds in 4:32 is instructive and is likely an allusion to one of several OT texts depicting the eschatological ingathering of gentiles (Judg 9:15; Ps 104:12; Ezek 17:23; 31:6; Dan 4:12). Taken together, the reception of gentiles in the Jewish homeland, Jesus's boundary-breaking ministry, and Jesus's teaching on the kingdom all foreshadow the inauguration of the gentile mission.

The gentile mission formally begins in 5:1–20 with the deliberate movement into gentile territory. There, in perhaps the most extensive exorcism in the NT, Jesus heals a man possessed by a legion of demons (5:9). Though it has already been suggested that the scene functions within a larger narrative context (4:35—5:43), the passage also contributes to Mark's gentile mission. The foray into gentile territory (the region of the Gerasenes [5:1]) marks the first time that Jesus has ventured outside the Jewish homeland. In many respects, the account parallels Jesus's activities in the Jewish homeland. Just as the Jewish mission begins with an exorcism, so too does the gentile mission begin with the healing of a possessed man (1:21–28; 5:1–20).

In addition to this parallel, the scene also appears to have a preparatory function. What begins as a story about Jesus's compassion for an individual concludes on a note that has broader implication for the gentiles. The presence of a large herd of swine (an unclean animal according to Jewish tradition [Lev 11:7; Deut 14:8]) indicates that Jesus is in gentile territory and that the region is defiled. That the confrontation ends with the swine being drowned in the sea—perhaps distasteful to modern sensibilities—communicates the demonic expulsion from the man and the surrounding territory.

The first gentile journey paves the way for the second journey into gentile territory in 7:24—8:9, a sequence involving three distinct scenes. After arriving in the region of Tyre, Jesus is approached by a Syrophoenician woman whose daughter is demon possessed (7:24–30). The scene is unusual in that Jesus appears to deny the women's request to heal her daughter: "Let the children be fed first, for it is not fair to take the children's food and throw it to the dogs" (7:27). Though it seems as if Jesus has rebuffed the woman's request, it may be that there is more to this response than meets the eye (or ear). To appreciate this statement, it is necessary to situate the response within the broader narrative context. The audience knows that Jesus has already received gentiles (like the Syrophoenician woman) in the Jewish homeland (3:7–12) and that Jesus has already engaged in a ministry among gentiles (5:1–20). In view of this context, it may be that Jesus's response is a kind of test according to the new standards of purity (7:18–23). That the woman is able to understand the statement, much less interpret it and extend the parable, is evidence of her genuine faith and purity.

Although the episode involves the healing of the woman's daughter, the dialogue between Jesus and the Syrophoenician woman exposes an important theological theme in the narrative. The Jewish people are the "children" of God, and Jesus's ministry prioritizes a mission to the Jewish people. However, such a mission is not at the exclusion of gentiles for whom Jesus repeatedly demonstrates love and compassion. Gentiles may also partake of the blessings associated with Jesus's ministry. In narrative terms, the gentiles may not be "first" (7:27), but even "the dogs under the table eat the children's crumbs" (7:28).

This theological summary is reaffirmed in the concluding scenes of the second gentile journey. From Tyre, Jesus and the disciples depart to the region of the Decapolis (7:31–37) where they encounter a deaf man with a speech impediment. As has been the case in similar episodes, the healing of the man demonstrates Jesus's power and authority over disease. But given the placement of the episode at this juncture of the narrative, the healing also accentuates that gentiles have "ears to hear" (cf. 4:9). This receptivity once again parallels the response to Jesus among those in the Jewish homeland.

In the final scene of the second journey (8:1–9), Jesus once again interacts with a large crowd who has been with him for an extended period of time and is without food. For the second time in Mark's narrative (cf. 6:33–44), Jesus multiplies loaves and fishes to satisfy the crowd, in this case numbering four thousand (8:9). Although the two feeding accounts are similar, the primary difference is that the first feeding takes place in Jewish territory, while the second is in gentile territory. The deliberate plotting of episodes emphasizes the prioritization in Jesus's ministry, while at the same time demonstrating his love for all people (cf. 7:27; Rom 1:16). The parallel accounts further illustrate Jesus's compassion for both Jew and gentile alike.

The third journey into gentile territory (8:22—9:29) continues to reiterate similar themes as Jesus heals a blind man and a demon-possessed boy (9:14–29). In addition to the healings, it is on the third journey that Peter identifies Jesus as the Messiah (8:29) and that Jesus is transfigured on the mountain (9:2–13). The placement of these revelatory scenes—in gentile territory no less—appears to be a deliberate narrative move. The final journey is notable in that it is among gentiles that Jesus first permits *anyone* to follow him, so long as they are willing to deny themselves and take up their cross (8:34).

The gentile journeys come to a close in 9:29, but the theme of inclusion carries forward into the passion narrative. There are no more healings or exorcisms, but there is a concerted effort to reintegrate the geopolitical spaces mentioned at the beginning of the narrative. Just as individuals from Galilee, Judea, and the neighboring gentile regions flocked to Jesus in 3:7–8, so too is Jesus surrounded by representatives from similar regions in the passion. Simon of Cyrene (North Africa) carries Jesus's cross (15:21); women from Galilee, including Mary Magdalene, Mary the mother of James, and Salome observe the crucifixion (15:40–41, 47) and go to the tomb (16:1–2); and Joseph of Arimathea (Judea) petitions Pilate for the body of Jesus after he dies

(15:42–46). Each of these figures fills in for the disciples (14:50) and becomes a servant of Jesus in his hour of need.

Perhaps the most unexpected character to respond to Jesus in the passion narrative is the centurion responsible for overseeing the crucifixion. Immediately after Jesus dies, the centurion declares, "Truly this man was God's Son!" (15:39). The statement is remarkable both because it is found on the lips of a gentile and because it represents the only full recognition of Jesus's identity by a human character in the narrative. The scene is strikingly similar to the baptism when the heavens are torn and Jesus is declared to be God's Son (1:10–11). This time, however, when the temple veil is torn (15:38), it is not the divine voice speaking but a gentile who utters the declaration.

Mark's depiction of Jesus and the careful plotting of the narrative communicates a deliberate concern for those beyond the boundaries of the Jewish homeland. Jesus's reception of gentiles, as well as the repeated journeys into gentile territory, emphasize his compassion and love for those beyond the Jewish homeland. This radical inclusion is not to suggest a rejection or turning away from the Jewish people, but rather a reorienting of the kingdom that is broader, more diverse, and more inclusive than was likely embraced by some within and beyond Mark's community.

Service and Suffering

The second half of Mark's Gospel moves toward the crucifixion. Accordingly, there is a strong emphasis on service and suffering. Though the theme comes into sharp relief in the latter portion of the narrative, it is evident throughout Mark's story. This may seem antithetical to Jesus's display of power and authority, but the two work in a complementary fashion and animate Jesus's ministry across the narrative.

The story of Jesus's death takes place in Mark 14–15, but the narrative moves steadily towards the crucifixion from the very beginning. In Jesus's first encounter with the religious leaders, he is accused of blasphemy (2:7)—the same charge for which he will be deemed worthy of death at the Jewish trial (14:61–64). In 2:19 when Jesus is asked why his disciples do not fast, he responds by observing that "days will come when the bridegroom is taken away from them" (2:20). Though cryptic, this appears to be the first reference to Jesus's impending death in Mark's narrative. Additional clarity is offered in the next chapter when Jesus heals a man with a withered hand (3:1–6). The response prompts the Pharisees to begin conspiring with the Herodians "to destroy him" (3:6)—a more explicit reference to Jesus's looming death. In 3:13–19 Jesus calls the twelve disciples. Among the list of names, the narrator identifies Judas Iscariot as the one who "betrayed him" (3:19). While there is no indication how Judas is to betray Jesus nor how all of these pieces might fit together, the clues set an ominous trajectory that foreshadows the final, tragic events of Mark's story.

This movement towards the passion gains momentum as the story continues to unfold. In chs. 8, 9, and 10, Jesus explicitly predicts that he will suffer and die. Although there is slight variation between the predictions (8:31; 9:31; 10:32–34), the basic components are repeated across all three scenes: 1) Jesus will be delivered into the hands of men, 2) Jesus will be put to death, and 3) Jesus will rise from the dead three days later. In 8:31 and 10:32–34, Jesus indicates that the religious leaders will play a decisive role, with the caveat in 10:32–34 that he will be put to death specifically by the gentiles.

The Jewish leadership play a significant role in Jesus's death. Though a wise scribe is "not far from the kingdom of

God" (12:34) and Joseph of Arimathea—a member of the Jewish council—identifies with Jesus after his death (15:42–46), there is a pervasive and building tension between Jesus and the religious leadership. The essence of this conflict is narrated in Mark 12:1–12. There Jesus speaks a parable about a vineyard and tenants (cf. Isa 5:1–7). Though there is much debate about the parable, the scene symbolically depicts the religious leaders' hostility and rejection of God's beloved Son, Jesus.

The final chapters of Mark's Gospel describe the arrest, trial, crucifixion, and burial of Jesus. Though scholars vigorously debate why Jesus dies in the second Gospel (see the discussion at the end of the chapter), there is little doubt that suffering and service are intertwined in Mark. The ideas are implicitly joined at various places but the clearest statement occurs in Mark 10:42–45. In a passage clarifying the nature of kingdom-centered leadership, the Markan Jesus responds to the disciples' misguided perspective:

> You know that among the Gentiles those whom they recognize as their rulers lord it over them, and their great ones are tyrants over them. But it is not so among you; but whoever wishes to become great among you must be your servant, and whoever wishes to be first among you must be slave of all. For the Son of Man came not to be served but to serve, and to give his life a ransom for many. (10:42–45)

The statement is, in part, a response to James and John who petition Jesus to sit at his right and left (10:37)—a request that likely conveys their own skewed understanding of Jesus as well as their own desire for positions of power. However, true greatness is not derived from titles, offices, or worldly positions but rather in service to others. In God's kingdom the "first will be last, and the last will be first"

(10:31; cf. 9:35). Jesus therefore flips the script and offers a countercultural ethic that is intended to characterize all would-be followers.

This ethic is not a principle that originates out of theoretical abstraction. It is rooted in the ministry of Jesus (10:45), a ministry exemplified by the good shepherd's love and compassion (cf. 6:34). This benevolent service is illustrated in Jesus's mighty deeds, which are a prominent feature in the first half of the Gospel. But the quintessential expression of this service is exemplified in the giving of Jesus's life as a "ransom for many" (10:45). When viewed holistically, Jesus's interactions throughout the Gospel communicate his gracious service and provide a model of discipleship for all who are willing to "deny themselves and take up their cross" (8:34).

Jesus's suffering and service define his mission and provide a lens through which to understand his authority and power. Unlike those who are recognized as rulers of this world, using their authority to advance their own self-interests (10:42), the Markan Jesus wields power for the betterment of others. He heals the sick (e.g., 1:29–31, 40–45; 3:1–6), exorcises the possessed (e.g., 1:21–28; 5:1–20; 7:24–30), forgives sin (2:1–12), and pours out his blood for the many (14:24). His ministry is characterized by a selfless concern for the physical and spiritual restoration of others, regardless of the cost.

To this end, Mark's Jesus makes no distinction among supplicants. He heals those who are marginalized (5:25–34) just as he does the social elite (5:21–24, 35–43). He does not discriminate based on status or reputation (2:15–17), but advocates for those deemed outcasts by society. He is not partial to individuals with social/political standing or even to those who might advance his own reputation (8:11–13). Indeed, the Markan Jesus reserves his most direct and withering critique to those recognized as earthly leaders (7:1–13; 10:2–12; 12:1–12), demonstrating an indifference to the perception of others.

This attitude of service, which dictates Jesus's use of authority and power, must be understood within the context of Jesus's relationship to the Father. His God-given authority (1:11; 9:7; 11:28–33) is exercised not for the advancement of his own agenda, but in service to the Father's plan. Throughout the narrative, Jesus's devotion to God is unwavering. Even as he faces the inevitability of the cross (8:31), anguishing over the cup before him, Jesus reaffirms his commitment to the Father: "Remove this cup from me; yet, not what I want, but what you want" (14:36). This kingdom-first perspective motivates Jesus's deeds and differentiates him from all other brokers of power in Mark's Gospel.

In view of this, it is important to recognize that Jesus's power and authority, coupled with his suffering and death, are two sides of the same coin. Historically, some have struggled to appreciate how these perspectives can be reconciled: a powerful Jesus who wields control over sickness and death *and* a suffering Jesus who is not able to carry his own cross and dies in the face of complete abandonment. Some have argued that the Markan narrative presents divergent christological perspectives that have been haphazardly joined together. Others have suggested that Mark evidences a "corrective" Christology that knowingly pits these competing perspectives against one another. Though it must be acknowledged that Jesus's deeds of power seem far removed from his suffering and death, the characterization of Jesus is remarkably consistent across the narrative. The Markan Jesus heals the broken and dies on a cross *in order to serve the many*. Neither piece of the equation is intended to "correct" the other, just as neither stands in contradiction to the other. In the end, Mark's depiction of Jesus evidences a faithfulness to the great commandment: to love God and to love others (12:29–31). Though his love and compassion take on different forms at different points in the narrative, they are animated by an attitude of service to the divine plan.

JESUS'S RELATIONSHIP TO GOD

The discussion thus far has considered several defining characteristics of Mark's Jesus. These include his unique power and authority, his love and compassion for all people, and his suffering and service. Having offered a broad portrayal of Jesus based on Mark's narrative, the conversation now turns to a more contested issue. Is the Markan Jesus a human figure who serves as an agent of God? Is he divine? Or is he to be identified as the God of Israel?

Assessing these questions reveals what has often been described as a "low" or "high" Christology. A "low" Christology affirms that Jesus, though designated Messiah and Son of God, is an ordinary human figure who acts on God's behalf. He is imbued with power, but his miraculous works come from God. He is not a god or Israel's God. He is a human figure with a special relationship to God who acts as God's ambassador throughout the narrative.

In contrast, a "high" Christology is associated with a range of views that, broadly speaking, understand Jesus to be a transcendent figure. For some, Jesus is to be likened to one of the Greco-Roman gods. Others assert that Jesus is the functional equivalent of God in the narrative. Still others go a step further and argue that Jesus is to be equated with Israel's God. Though there is significant variance between these "high" christological perspectives, they are bound together by the idea that Jesus is a participant in the divine sphere.

It should be acknowledged that not only is this an important discussion among scholars, but it bears relevance for people of faith. Following the ecumenical councils of the fourth and fifth centuries, the church has traditionally affirmed that Jesus is fully human and fully divine. Because this perspective has been baked into the tradition over the last fifteen hundred years, many assume that the creeds reflect the earliest traditions about Jesus, extending all the way back to the Gospels. The implicit reasoning goes, therefore, that Mark's Gospel (or any NT text for that matter) *must* convey a "high" Christology. Indeed, to think anything less would be heretical.

This approach is understandable, but there are at least three issues that complicate the discussion. First, many assume that the distinction between a low and high Christology is essentially a choice between bad vs. good or wrong vs. right. Admittedly, the nomenclature is open to confusion as the terms set up a comparative and potentially oppositional framework. But this is not the intent of the terminology and such ideas should not be assumed.

Second, the notion that Jesus is fully divine and/or coequal with the Father is a theological construct that developed over a significant period of time. The discussions around these ideas and their resultant clarification were communicated hundreds of years after Mark was composed. Although the ancient creeds and councils have become the standard by which Christians confess Jesus, it may be anachronistic to apply these to Mark. If the second Gospel is to be appreciated in its own sociohistorical context (as it should), projecting these doctrines onto the narrative may skew or even distort the text. One should not assume that Mark held the same theological perspective or was even interested in the same theological concerns that emerged as a result of controversies that developed *after* the first century.

Third, even if it should be determined that Mark reflects a low Christology, such a view is not to be regarded as problematic for people of faith. Mark's Gospel was written at a particular historical moment some forty years after the Christ event. During this time, the early church began to consider and to describe who Jesus was. Many of their conceptions are expressed in the documents we now call the NT. It needs to be emphasized that this was a communal process orchestrated over a period of time, not a momentary reflection by a single individual (how could one person possibly capture and communicate the mysteries of the exalted Christ?). The author of Mark was a participant in this activity and can be located somewhere along this developmental journey. That Mark may not have described Jesus using language adopted by Christians in the fourth century only underscores the author's own situatedness.

All of this is to say that interpreters should approach Mark with an open mind. This requires giving careful attention to Mark's narrative, respecting the author's voice and place within the canon, and resisting the urge to import later theological assertions onto Mark's story of Jesus. This may be difficult for those who identify as Christian and whose perceptions of Jesus have been shaped by creeds and councils that took place over a millennium ago. However, any attempt to understanding Jesus must begin with the unique and manifold witness of the NT, including the Gospel of Mark.

These preliminary observations aside, the following discussion will explore the relationship between Jesus and God. It will be shown that Mark's narrative points in different directions and contributes to both a low and high

Christology. Relevant texts and common arguments are surveyed below before offering a few observations by way of conclusion.

Low Christology

Few, if any, would dispute the idea that Mark's Jesus is human. He walks, talks, eats, and expresses emotion like other characters. He has "brothers" and "sisters" and is recognized as a carpenter (6:3–4). When his deeds become public, some inquire about his identity and he is invariably likened to earthly figures such as John the Baptist, Elijah, or one of the prophets (6:14–15). There is little doubt that Jesus is portrayed as human. However, because Jesus is portrayed with humanlike qualities, the question is whether he is *only* human. For those advocating a low Christology, several arguments are frequently advanced in support of this conclusion.

Scholars often note that Mark places particular emphasis on Jesus's earthly life. There is no virgin birth or infancy story like Matthew or Luke (Matt 1:18; Luke 1:35), nor is there any indication that Jesus is a preexistent being who was "in the beginning with God" (John 1:2). The Markan Jesus arrives on the scene as an adult with no mention of his birth or pre-birth status. In contrast to the other Gospels, the characterization of Jesus in Mark's Gospel focuses on his earthy existence. Thus, to assert that Jesus is divine or superhuman reaches beyond the narrative and is dependent on ideas that are foreign to the second Gospel.

It has also been observed that Mark's Jesus displays certain human limitations. For example, although Jesus discusses future events, even he must admit that his knowledge is incomplete: "No one knows [the hour], neither the angels in heaven, nor the Son, but only the Father" (13:32). This candid admission seems to dovetail with what, at times, appears to be a limited display of power. After Jesus returns to his hometown (6:1–6), the narrator states that Jesus "could do no deed of power there, except that he laid his hands on a few sick people and cured them" (6:5). The narrator indicates that Jesus was amazed at the people's lack of faith (6:6), a comment that has sometimes been interpreted to be the reason for Jesus's inability. However, this is an inference that has likely been adopted from the Gospel of Matthew (Matt 15:54–58).

Along these lines, one might also note the two-stage healing in Mark 8:22–26 where Jesus heals a blind man. Although the healing of a physical ailment is not unusual, what is striking is the circuitous path of restoration. After Jesus spits on the man's eyes (spittle was regarded as an aid to healing by many in the ancient world), the man begins to see. However, his vision is still blurred (8:24) and it is only after a second touch that he is able to see clearly (8:25). Though the two-stage healing likely has a broader function—signifying the disciples' partial understanding and need for a second restorative touch—the scene has been understood by some to indicate a defect in Jesus's powers, similar to the episode in 6:1–6.

Thus, both in his knowledge and power Mark's Jesus is circumscribed by earthly restrictions that differentiate him from the divine. There are, of course, instances where Jesus displays authority over creation. That is not a question. At issue is which texts have interpretive priority. Those adopting a low Christology argue that interpreters cannot minimize and/or ignore episodes in which Jesus's power is constrained. In fact, these episodes ought to be the lens by which the broader discussion is framed.

If this is the case, then Jesus is not to be regarded as an individual with divine status, but as a person having a unique and intimate relationship with God. Jesus is a human agent through whom God's power and mercy are expressed in the narrative. He is adopted as God's "Son" at the baptism (1:9–11) in the same way that Israel or its kings were designated as sons of God. Jesus is a human character who has been commissioned for God's service and given authority to fulfill God's purposes.

To this end, the narrator intentionally distinguishes Jesus from God. A variety of passages point in this direction. Consider the opening verses of Mark's Gospel: "As it is written in the prophet Isaiah, 'See, I am sending my messenger ahead of you, who will prepare your way; "Prepare the way of the Lord, make his paths straight"'" (1:2–3). In Mark, this passage refers specifically to the ministry of John the Baptist and Jesus. Although several OT texts are merged together here (Exod 23:20; Mal 3:1; Isa 40:3), Mark lays particular emphasis on the Isaianic reference ("Prepare the way of the Lord, make his paths straight" [Isa 40:3]). In the context of Isaiah, it is notable that this preparatory work is to be done in anticipation of *God's arrival*. But Mark has modified the quotation so that God is the speaker and Jesus is the coming one. This distinction is important and signals to the audience that Mark's Jesus and God are *different* characters, even if the work of Jesus is closely aligned with the activity of God.

Various other texts seem to cohere with this depiction. For example, in 12:35–37 Jesus inquires why the teachers of the law suggest that the Messiah is the son of David since David declares, "The Lord said to my Lord" (12:36). There are numerous elements of contention in this passage (e.g., whether Davidic messianism is affirmed or rejected). However, the key issue for the present discussion is the differentiation between Jesus and God. The same delineation is observable in 6:46 and 14:32 when Jesus prays to God.

Though it seems fairly obvious that Jesus is not praying to himself *as* God, any uncertainty is removed when Jesus addresses his prayer to "Abba, Father" (14:36) in the garden of Gethsemane. That Jesus is not the Father or one with the Father is implicitly affirmed on the cross, when Jesus cries out "Eloi, Eloi, lema sabachthani?," which being translated means, "My God, my God, why have you forsaken me?" (15:34).

Perhaps the most explicit passage highlighting the distinction between Jesus and God occurs in Mark 10:17–22. There Jesus encounters a rich young ruler who is concerned about obtaining eternal life. As the man approaches, he kneels, addresses Jesus as "Good Teacher" and inquires about the necessary requirements to inherit eternal life. Before taking up the question Jesus first responds with a question and assertion of his own, "Why do you call me good? No one is good but God alone" (10:18). This response is highly significant as it reiterates the basic distinction between Jesus and God. It further insinuates that there is an ontological distinction between the two. The Markan Jesus rejects being equated with God since the Father alone can be described as good.

This differentiation between Jesus and God may seem foreign to modern Christians, but many have argued that the depiction is thoroughly Jewish. Mark's portrayal of Jesus, as well as the corresponding portrait of God, aligns with an understanding of Jewish monotheism. One of the foundational tenants of the Jewish faith was a belief that YHWH was the one and only God. This theological affirmation is rooted in numerous OT texts, but none more important than Deut 6:4: "Hear, O Israel: The Lord our God, the Lord is one." Known as the *Shema* (Hebrew "to hear"), this passage was regularly recited by Jewish people and was a cornerstone of the faith. Since Mark is written from a

Jewish perspective, it seems only natural that the narrative would reflect a monotheistic outlook. This is a reasonable deduction for religious and cultural reasons, but it is also noteworthy that Jesus explicitly affirms the *Shema* (12:29). All of this is to suggest that Mark's low Christology, far from being a theological deficiency, would have presented the community with a more palatable portrayal of Jesus, given the Gospel's Jewish roots.

Based on the totality of evidence, many have argued that Mark presents a low Christology. Jesus is a character with otherworldly power but only as a result of God's empowerment. He is nowhere described as a preexistent being or equal with God. His relationship to God is unlike any of the other characters in the narrative, but he is the son of a carpenter (6:3) who is used by God for kingdom service.

High Christology

Unlike the position outlined above, others maintain that Mark's Jesus is more than human—whether that be a supernatural being, a man who is deified, God's divine Son, or even the God of Israel. This high Christology includes various permutations, but several common arguments undergird the discussion.

A number of passages seemingly associate Jesus with the divine. Consider three episodes in particular. At first blush, Mark 2:1–12 is a typical miracle story: a supplicant is brought to or appears before Jesus, the individual is restored, and the onlookers respond in amazement. However, the scene in 2:1–12 is different. The healing of the paralytic comes after a controversy that emerges between Jesus and the teachers of the law. The conflict arises when Jesus, having witnessed the actions of the man's friends, declares, "Your sins are forgiven" (2:5).

In and of itself this may seem like an unremarkable statement as Jewish priests regularly offered forgiveness. But there is categorical difference in Mark's depiction. Whereas priests extended forgiveness as a response to confession and an offering, Jesus initiates forgiveness out of his perception of the human heart. As such, by offering forgiveness to the man, Jesus appears to take on divine prerogatives. The shocking nature of Jesus's pronouncement is confirmed by the religious leaders who accuse him of blasphemy since no one "can forgive sins but God alone" (2:7). Though Jesus does not address this statement directly, he seemingly disputes the charge (2:8–10) before offering a word of healing to validate his divine authority.

Second, a similar association occurs in the stilling of the storm as Jesus and the disciples make their way across the sea (4:35–41). As mentioned above, the passage highlights the characterization of Jesus as one with authority and power. Scholars have long observed that the episode shares similarities with the Jonah narrative. In both accounts, a storm develops on the sea (Jonah 1:4; Mark 4:37), which poses a danger for those on board (Jonah 1:4; Mark 4:37). As the storm rages, both Jonah (Jonah 1:5) and Jesus (Mark 4:38) are asleep in the boat. The perilous situation prompts a dismayed captain to wake Jonah (Jonah 1:6), just as the disciples rouse a sleeping Jesus (Mark 4:38). In the end, the threatening storm subsides (Jonah 1:15; Mark 4:39), causing the sailors, like the disciples, to respond in fear (Jonah 1:16; Mark 4:41). In view of these similarities, many affirm that Mark deliberately echoes the Jonah narrative.

However, there is one striking difference between the accounts that may shed light on the purpose of the allusion. In Jonah, the prophet is awakened during the chaotic storm in order that he might pray (Jonah 1:6)—the assumption being that only a deity can exercise control over the wind and sea. But in Mark Jesus makes no attempt to pray. Instead, he simply commands the wind and sea to "be quiet" (4:39). The implication seems to be that the Markan Jesus is not a mere mortal who is dependent on prayer. *Jesus is like God* who alone is sovereign over the created order. While the disciples do not understand, Mark prompts the audience to consider the deeper meaning, albeit through a question posed by the disciples: "Who then is this, that even the wind and the sea obey him?" (4:41).

A third text illustrating Mark's high Christology occurs in 6:45–52. Similar to the previous example, the passage in question involves a sea crossing. This time, however, Jesus sends the disciples before him to the other side of the sea (6:45–46). During the night, while the disciples are straining at the oars, a water-walking Jesus approaches and is about "to pass them by" (6:48). When the disciples see the figure walking on the water, they mistakenly think that Jesus is a ghost and become terrified (6:49–50). The scene concludes when Jesus identifies himself, enters the boat, and the winds subside (6:50–51).

Once again, Mark's depiction is enriched by a surplus of meaning via the multiple references to the OT. To begin, the broad portrayal of Jesus is noteworthy since only God is able to make a pathway through the sea (Job 9:8; 38:16; Ps 77:19; Isa 43:16). In addition, that Jesus was about to "pass" by (6:48) may seem like a strange and incidental detail (perhaps even rude), but it echoes conceptions of deity found in the OT (e.g., Exod 33:22; 1 Kgs 19:11). In such instances, God is described as passing by an individual (i.e., Moses or Elijah) in an act of self-revelation. This interpretive trajectory is further supported by Jesus's identification as "I am" (6:50). The affirmation recalls the disclosure of the divine name in Exodus (Exod 3:14) and deepens the christological portrait by drawing yet another correspondence between

Jesus and God. When viewed holistically, these interlocking references closely align the activities and speech of Jesus with Israel's God.

This type of allusive association extends to another curious detail in Mark's narrative—the ambiguous use of κύριος (Lord). In the Greek translation of the OT, the designation κύριος is frequently used in place of YHWH, the name of Israel's God (e.g., Gen 2:8; Exod 3:4; Lev 1:1; Num 20:9; Deut 10:1). But in Mark the term κύριος is used in an interesting fashion. Though the second Gospel affirms that there is only one Lord (12:29), one κύριος, the title is sometimes used with what appears to be deliberate ambiguity.

Consider the OT citation in 1:2–3. While some have interpreted these verses as affirming the fundamental distinction between Jesus and God, the issue is slightly more complex.

> As it is written in the prophet Isaiah, "See, I am sending my messenger ahead of you, who will prepare **your** way; the voice of one crying out in the wilderness: 'Prepare the way of the **Lord**, make his paths straight.'" (Mark 1:2–3)

At issue is the pronoun "your" in v. 2 and the term "Lord" in v. 3. Who exactly are the referents of these terms? Whose way or ways are being prepared? Although some have interpreted v. 2 (i.e., "your") in reference to Jesus and v. 3 (i.e., "Lord") in reference to God, others have suggested that this approach is misguided. The opening of the Gospel (1:1) identifies Jesus as the main protagonist, and the following verses depict John as the one who prepares the way (1:4–8). If this is correct, then Jesus is the most natural way to understand the identity of the κύριος in v. 3—the name typically reserved for Israel's God. Such an interpretation is subtle but it may reflect another attempt to associate Jesus and God.

A similar phenomenon occurs in Mark 5:1–20. After Jesus expels the "legion" of demons, the man who had been demon possessed requests to go with him (5:18). Jesus instead instructs the man to "[g]o home to your friends, and tell them how much the Lord has done for you, and what mercy he has shown you" (5:19). The concluding verse of the episode states that the man "went away and began to proclaim in the Decapolis how much Jesus had done for him" (5:20). Once again there is an understated but important theological issue in the concluding two verses. Jesus instructs the man to go home and announce all that the κύριος (Lord) has done for him (5:19). However, the man returns home and speaks of all that Jesus has done for him (5:20). The shift from κύριος in v. 19 to Jesus in v. 20 is intriguing. Does the use of κύριος in 5:19 refer to God, to Jesus, or both? Admittedly, it is not clear.

It does not appear that this kind of ambiguity arises from a careless or unskilled narrator. When appreciated within the broader framework of Mark's story, the ambiguity appears deliberate. The narrative does not pause to explain the implications of the association, but the audience recognizes that there is something theological being affirmed about Jesus. Such an association raises the possibility that Jesus is a divine figure or perhaps even God. Ironically, though the religious leaders do not believe that Jesus is divine, they seemingly acknowledge this implication based upon his activities (2:5–7). The perception that Jesus is claiming something more appears to be why he is ultimately convicted by the Jewish authorities (14:61–65).

If this interpretation is correct, it raises the question of how to understand Mark in light of Jewish monotheism. Two passages (12:28–34; 12:35–37) weigh upon the conversation. In 12:28–34, Jesus is asked about the greatest commandment. His response, as noted, is significant because the Markan Jesus explicitly affirms the *Shema* and the oneness of God. The second passage (12:35–37) deals with the relationship between the Christ and David (Ps 110). The latter passage is particularly significant since Jesus identifies two κύριοι (i.e., Lords) around the divine throne ("The Lord said to my Lord, 'Sit at my right hand, until I put your enemies under your feet'" [Mark 12:36]). As noted above, Mark 12:35–37 appears to distinguish Jesus from God. However, the same passage also affirms Jesus *alongside* God as a second κύριος. The question then becomes how can these potentially conflicting texts be reconciled?

There are, of course, various ways to handle these issues but some have argued that the two passages affirm both a high Christology and God's oneness. Assuming that Mark is a capable author, it seems that the juxtaposition of these passages is not an irreconcilable paradox. On the one hand, Mark upholds monotheism. In fact, Mark is the only author to quote the *Shema* in the fourfold Gospel tradition (cf. Matt 22:34–40; Luke 10:25–28). On the other hand, the narrative uses terminology that exalts Mark's Jesus, drawing direct parallels with Israel's God. It may be that an affirmation of the *Shema* in 12:28–34 is not incompatible with the two κύριοι in 12:35–37.

Other studies have seemingly opened the door for this line of interpretation. More recent work has suggested that Jewish monotheism was not so rigid as to disallow the possibility of other divine figures, even divine intermediaries. Some have argued, for example, that during the Second Temple period there was a belief in "two powers." Others maintain that God's word and wisdom were viewed as distinct realities within the divine sphere. The takeaway is that there was not a fixed view of God's oneness but rather a degree of flexibility in how Jewish people understood monotheism. It is possible then to affirm both the evolutionary development of Mark's Christology as well as its connection to a monotheistic perspective.

In sum, Mark's Jesus is no ordinary human being. He is not another devout individual or agent of God. He calms the storms, walks on water, and is suggestively linked to the κύριος. Whether this close association indicates that Jesus is a divine being or shares in the identity of God remains a matter of debate. According to some scholars, what can be affirmed is that the Markan Jesus transcends the natural world and encroaches on the divine.

Reflections

After considering arguments for both positions, the curious student will wonder how scholars can arrive at these divergent perspectives. How does the same narrative seemingly communicate such distinct messages about the person of Jesus, the central character of the story? Individual presuppositions and faith commitments have a strong bearing on interpretive decisions (or any text for that matter). Yet there may be something more elemental driving these perspectives.

Part of the challenge associated with interpreting Mark is due to the rhetoric of the narrative. That is, the way in which Mark's story is told affects how the story is understood. Mark's narrative frequently employs implicit techniques in the characterization of Jesus. Because the story is communicated in this fashion, the audience is required to actively make connections that are not explicit in the text itself. This is not to say that there are no direct statements about Jesus or that the story is so thoroughly cryptic that it cannot be deciphered. However, there are puzzles and paradoxes in the narrative that require unraveling.

The beauty of this approach is that it produces an inviting and engaging experience. The nuances and subtleties of the story entice the audience to actively participate in the meaning-making process. As the narrative web unfolds, the audience is pulled into the drama and the slew of rhetorical devices that invite reflection. The various subtleties, allusions, and complexities in the narrative add texture and depth and create an aesthetic experience that is filled with intrigue and suspense.

However, Mark's approach also comes with a challenge. The structuring of the story and the various allusions are crafted to serve the larger purpose of the Gospel, but these intentions are all too often unstated. The meaning of these elements must be supplied by the audience in the act of interpretation. Because interpreters are invariably shaped by their own experiences, how one understands these elements, how they fill in the unstated intentions, *can produce significantly different interpretations.*

Perhaps an analogy would be helpful to appreciate these narrative dynamics. Consider the following image (fig. 3.1). What do you see?

Figure 3.1

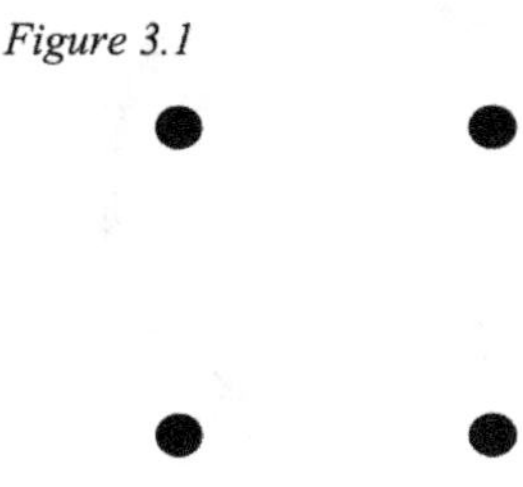

One could reply, "I see four dots." This, of course, is a correct answer. However, someone else might notice that the dots appear to be placed in a deliberate and structured pattern: two rows of two, spaced approximately equal distance from side to side and top to bottom. Someone might therefore respond by filling in the missing portions of the image. For example, "I see the outline of a square" (fig. 3.2).

Figure 3.2

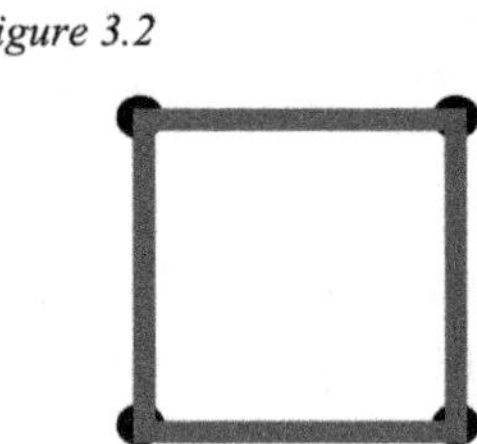

Still others could offer another permutation: "I see a circle" [fig. 3.3]). Indeed, because we are dealing with fragmentary information, though the data points are fixed, it is possible to fill out the image in any number of ways, all while beginning with the same elemental starting points.

Figure 3.3

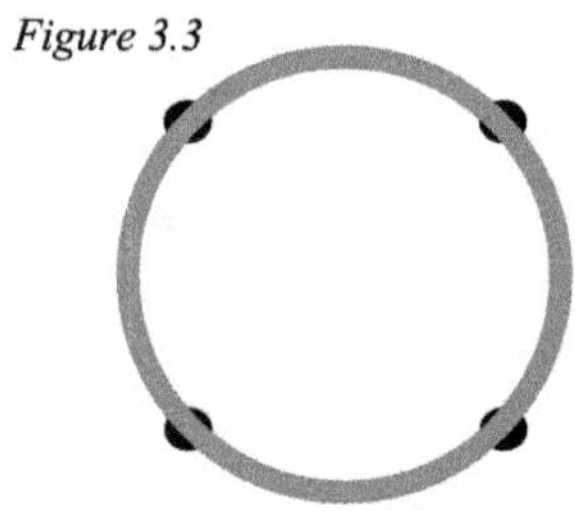

This is not unlike the second Gospel. The depiction of Jesus offers some fixed points of reference (e.g., Jesus is the Christ [1:1]), but there is much that is unstated. Is Jesus a human figure? Is he divine? Is he to be equated with God? Mark does not provide a direct answer to these questions. Scholars must fill in the proverbial gaps as part of the interpretive process. In this participatory activity, some see a square while others see a circle, even though they are examining the same narrative text.

In my own estimation, the two positions are not mutually exclusive. The narrative establishes the foundation for a low Christology by affirming Jesus's humanity. Yet the narrative frequently gestures to something beyond this. Jesus is a human figure but he is unlike the other human characters in the narrative. Whether through intertextual reference or allusive language—like waves cascading across a beach—the narrative repeatedly and deliberately pushes the audience to consider something more. Mark's explicitly low Christology is complemented by an implicitly high Christology that invites interpreters to consider Jesus's suprahuman status. For Mark, Jesus is the embodiment of the divine presence in the narrative and through whom God's inbreaking reign is inaugurated.

THE CRUCIFIXION

It goes without saying that Mark's crucifixion plays a pivotal role in the narrative. The last six chapters narrate the events leading up to and immediately after the crucifixion. But what does Mark want the audience to understand about the crucifixion? Why does Jesus die on the cross? Once again, simple answers elude us. The narrative does not offer a straightforward interpretation of Jesus's death. The significance of the event must be pieced together from the details of the narrative. In this final section of the chapter, two scholarly interpretations of Jesus's death will be considered.

Forgiveness of Sins

The first approach to Mark's crucifixion aligns with what many in the church typically assume is the primary function of Jesus's death. Jesus dies in order to forgive the debt incurred by humanity's sin. In support of this interpretation, scholars often point to two particular passages that shed light on the discussion.[1]

The first crucial text is Mark 10:45: "For the Son of Man came not to be served but to serve, and to give his life a ransom for many." This verse offers perhaps the most explicit statement about Jesus's death in the entire narrative. The saying, on the lips of Jesus, is located in the context of James and John's request to sit at Jesus's right and left (10:37). While the verse communicates something, what exactly does Mark mean by a "ransom"? And who or what are the many being ransomed from?

The concept of a ransom (either as a noun or a verb) is used numerous times in the OT. The term generally refers to the price or act of releasing and occurs in a number of diverse contexts, thus broadening the potential interpretive options. One could, for example, pay a ransom for the release of a prisoner captured in war (Isa 45:13), an Israelite who had been sold into slavery (Lev 25:51), or a portion of land (Lev 25:24).

Some have suggested that the closest conceptual antecedent to Mark occurs in passages like Exod 21 and 30. In Exod 21:28–32, the writer lays out the legal practice in the event that an individual is gored by a bull. If the goring

---

1. Collins, "Mark's Interpretation"; France, *Gospel of Mark*, 419–21; Watts, *Isaiah's New Exodus*, 349–62; Marcus, *Way of the Lord*, 195.

results in the death of an individual, the bull shall be put to death by stoning. No further action is to be taken against the owner of the bull, if the death was an unforeseeable accident. If the bull previously acted in a similar manner and the owner failed to take appropriate safeguards, the bull and the owner shall be put to death. However, the relatives of the deceased may request a "ransom" from the owner of the bull in exchange for the owner's life. The resulting payment could take any number of forms, including money, personal property, etc. A similar type of ransom is described in Exod 30:11–16, albeit in the context of a census and a payment required by every Israelite. The purpose of the ransom (Exod 30:16) was "to make atonement" for the Israelites who were numbered in the census (Exod 30:15) and needed to be redeemed by God from the penalty of death. Though the particulars differ in these two passages, the ransom is a payment made on behalf of and for the life of a liable party.

With this conceptual backdrop, many scholars interpret Mark's ransom saying in a similar fashion. Jesus came to give his life as a ransom—a form of payment—in exchange for the many. Though Mark does not state how "the many" offended God, it is assumed that the ransom is necessitated by human sin. Such a message falls in line with early church teaching and has a foothold in Mark's narrative. Recall that John the Baptist—Jesus's forerunner—came preaching a baptism of repentance for "the forgiveness of sins" (1:4). Introduced at the beginning of the narrative, the underlying problem of human sin is definitively addressed in and through Jesus's death. The ransom is not a monetary payment but the very giving of Jesus's life to redeem humanity from sin.

The second passage of significance is Mark 14:24. The scene is the Passover where Jesus declares that the cup is "my blood of the covenant, which is poured out for many" (14:24). Like Mark 10:45, the text makes reference to Jesus's death ("my blood . . . poured out") and the "many." Yet the concept of blood being poured out adds an additional layer of interpretation. This imagery, alluded to in Mark 14:24, occurs four times in Lev 4 (4:7, 18, 20, 25). There the author repeatedly uses the expression in relation to the pouring out of blood for "sin" (4:13, 14, 22, 26) or a "sin offering" (4:8, 20, 21, 24, 25). In this context, the blood sacrifice is intended to satisfy God in order to bring redemption for the guilty (4:26).

If these OT contexts are instructive, then the saying in 14:24 provides further reference to the covenantal and sacrificial nature of Jesus's death. By offering himself on the cross, Jesus becomes a sin offering for humanity ("the many"). Though the connection between these various ideas is not explicit, at least one interpreter of Mark follows this line of thinking. In the parallel passage in Matthew's Gospel, Jesus explicitly declares that the cup "is my blood of the covenant, which is poured out for many *for the forgiveness of sins*" (Matt 26:28, emphasis added).

For many people, this is the default explanation of Jesus's death. Jesus dies as a ransom in order to redeem humanity from the guilt and penalty of sin. The OT echoes that are embedded in the narrative provide the scriptural underpinnings for the interpretation of Mark's crucifixion. As a fuller articulation of this perspective, many point to Isaiah's suffering servant as a means of understanding Jesus's death in Mark.

> Surely he has borne our infirmities and carried our diseases; yet we accounted him stricken, struck down by God, and afflicted. But he was wounded for our transgressions, crushed for our iniquities; upon him was the punishment that

> made us whole, and by his bruises we are healed.
> All we like sheep have gone astray; we have all
> turned to our own way, and the LORD has laid on
> him the iniquity of us all. (Isa 53:4–6)

Liberation from Bondage

It bears repeating that Mark is notoriously reserved about the purpose of Jesus's death. Yes, Jesus dies. But why? In contrast to the traditional view, Malbon and Dowd argue that Jesus dies in order to bring liberation from demonic and human oppression.[2] Forgiveness is an aspect of the good news, but the death of Jesus has a broader theological function. How Malbon and Dowd arrive at this conclusion warrants consideration.

Malbon and Dowd begin by observing that there is no text in Mark that links the forgiveness of sins to the crucifixion. In fact, there are only two scenes where the term "sin" is used in Mark (1:4, 5; 2:5, 7, 9, 10). The first involves John the Baptist who proclaims "a baptism of repentance for the forgiveness of sins" (1:4). The second takes place in 2:1–12 when Jesus encounters a paralyzed man and proclaims his sins forgiven. In the first instance, there is no reference to Jesus or his death. In the second, the pronouncement comes during Jesus's earthly ministry and, once again, is not identified as being dependent on the crucifixion. To suggest, therefore, that Jesus's death is an atoning sacrifice seems at odds with a narrative that does not explicitly connect sin, forgiveness, and Jesus's death.

Like others, Malbon and Dowd identify 10:45 as key to understanding the meaning of Jesus's death. They are careful to observe that this verse should be interpreted through the lens of the narrative. As part of their narrative argument,

2. Malbon and Dowd, "Significance of Jesus' Death."

Malbon and Dowd locate the ransom saying within a segment that spans from 8:22 to 10:52 and is framed by two stories involving blind people (8:22–26; 10:46–52). In between these accounts, Mark narrates three passion predictions in which Jesus foreshadows his impending death (8:31; 9:31; 10:32–34). Each passion prediction is followed by a scene depicting the disciples' continued misunderstanding along with additional teaching material. The portrayal of the disciples is symbolically linked to the theme of blindness that begins and ends the section.

Malbon and Dowd argue that the broader frame is important for understanding Mark 10:45, though they first offer some brief reflections on the concept of a "ransom." As most would affirm, a ransom involves the release of those who have been "held captive or enslaved by another."[3] Of significance, however, is that in the context of the Greco-Roman world, a ransom was typically paid to an enemy, not a neutral party. To assert that Jesus's death is a payment to God (the traditional view) is at odds with the general usage of the term. Though proponents of this view frequently appeal to the OT, Malbon and Dowd argue that the ransom should be interpreted within its more widely accessible, cultural context.

If a ransom involves an enemy, who is the enemy in Mark's Gospel? According to Malbon and Dowd, there are two groups of enemies in Mark: human beings and unclean spiritual beings. The first group is represented by individuals who "lord" their authority over others and act as "tyrants" (10:42). The second group includes Satan and the demonic powers (3:20–30). Jesus is in conflict with both groups, but it is the second (Satan in particular) to whom the ransom is paid. In Mark, Satan is the chief adversary who opposes God's reign and oppresses humanity. Because

3. Malbon and Dowd, "Significance of Jesus' Death," 283.

of Satan's rule (and by extension the unclean spirits') the "shepherd" must be struck and condemned to death (14:27) in order to satisfy the demands of the strong man (3:27). This payment or ransom is made through Jesus's death and is offered as an act of service for humanity. Though in the end the resurrection will cheat Satan of his rightful payment, Jesus must endure the cross in order to liberate humanity from spiritual bondage.

Malbon and Dowd argue that this interpretation resonates with the narrative context (8:22—10:52), which emphasizes the exemplary nature of Jesus's death. Throughout the section, Mark underscores the theme of service to situate the passion predictions, while simultaneously connecting Jesus's self-gift with the call to discipleship (8:34–35; 9:35, 41; 10:21). "[W]hoever wishes to become great among you must be your servant, and whoever wishes to be first among you must be slave of all. For the Son of Man came not to be served but to serve, and to give his life a ransom for many" (10:43–45). For Malbon and Dowd, Mark's ransom saying must be understood within a paradigm of service that is set forth for all believers (8:34). The basis for this model is not dependent on an atoning sacrifice to redeem humanity from sin. Such an idea is foreign to the context and represents a non-repeatable act. Instead, the crucifixion models the kind of service-oriented life that is to characterize all would-be followers. As Jesus establishes a pattern of service that seeks to bring freedom and healing from the power of Satan, so too are disciples called to engage earthly "tyrants" who oppress the weak and vulnerable. Though these acts of service may be risky, believers are called to "take up their cross" (8:34) and follow the one who gave his life as a ransom for many.

In the end, Jesus's death must be interpreted within the context of Mark's narrative. Mark's story of Jesus does not connect the death of Jesus to the forgiveness of sins, but perhaps it proclaims a more powerful message: through Jesus's death, God has defeated the enemy and brought restoration to humanity.

Reflections

Two approaches to Jesus's death have been surveyed above. The traditional view maintains that Jesus's death is an atonement for sin. Malbon and Dowd argue that Jesus's death redeems humanity from the power of Satan.

While both views are attractive in certain respects, each succumbs to a similar problem. The traditional view does not cohere with a narrative that depicts Jesus forgiving sins during his earthly ministry. Although Malbon and Dowd attempt to situate the ransom within the context of the narrative, their literary reading also falters at the point of the narrative. Mark does not explicitly describe Jesus's death as a ransom to Satan, and one might argue that the narrative even resists such a notion.[4] Moreover, if the crucifixion is intended to bring liberation from the enemy, how does one explain the exorcisms in the narrative?—all of which take place before Jesus's death. And what is the interpreter to make of the fact that Jesus has already bound the strong man during his earthly ministry (3:27)?

In sum, what can be definitively stated is that Jesus's death is necessary and fulfills God's purposes. In Markan terms, it is a "ransom for many" (10:45). What this means is difficult to determine with any degree of certainty. Unfortunately, the narrative is too vague and too fragmentary

4. Mark's narrative seems to suggest that Satan opposes Jesus's death. This idea emerges from the first passion prediction where Peter is rebuked for his unwillingness to embrace the cross. Jesus's response—"Get behind me, Satan!" (8:33)—implies that Peter, like Satan, is opposed to the fulfillment of God's divine plan.

to push beyond the surface of the text. Perhaps the most we can affirm is that Jesus's death is an exemplary act of service for the benefit of others.[5]

CONCLUSION

This chapter has repeatedly shown that Mark's story of Jesus raises as many questions as it answers. Though the narrative deftly portrays Jesus's authority and power, his compassion for the marginalized, and his suffering and service, other features of the story are less transparent, including Jesus's relationship to God and the meaning of his death. The resulting christological portrait, which dances between revelation and concealment, is at once both elegantly simple and frustratingly complex. This rich interplay is provocatively inviting and tantalizes audiences to consider anew the person of Jesus. While the narrative may not satisfy the interpreter's every curiosity, it is sufficiently complete to answer for Mark what may be the most important question of all, "Who do you say that I am?" (8:29).

QUESTIONS FOR REFLECTION

1. How is Jesus depicted in the narrative? What are the foundational elements of Mark's Christology?

2. Which features of the narrative support a low Christology? Which affirm a high Christology?

3. Why does Jesus die in Mark's Gospel?

5. Reid, "Significance of the 'Ransom Saying.'"

FURTHER READING

Bird, Michael F. *Jesus among the Gods: Early Christology in the Greco-Roman World*. Waco, TX: Baylor University Press, 2022.

Collins, Adele Yarbro. "Mark's Interpretation of the Death of Jesus." *JBL* 128 (2009) 545–54.

Geddert, Timothy J. "The Implied YHWH Christology of Mark's Gospel: Mark's Challenge to the Reader to 'Connect the Dots.'" *BBR* 25 (2015) 325–40.

Johansson, Daniel. "*Kurios* in the Gospel of Mark." *JSNT* 33 (2010) 101–24.

———. "'Who Can Forgive Sins but God Alone?' Human and Angelic Agents, and Divine Forgiveness in Early Judaism." *JSNT* 33 (2011) 351–74.

Kirk, J. R. Daniel, ed. *Christology in Mark's Gospel: Four Views*. Critical Points. Grand Rapids: Zondervan, 2021.

———. *A Man Attested by God: The Human Jesus of the Synoptic Gospels*. Grand Rapids: Eerdmans, 2016.

Malbon, Elizabeth Struthers, and Sharyn Dowd. "The Significance of Jesus' Death in Mark: Narrative Context and Authorial Audience." *JBL* 125 (2006) 271–97.

Reid, Duncan. "The Significance of the 'Ransom Saying' in Mark 10:45." *CBQ* 84 (2022) 424–41.

Whitenton, Michael R. *Hearing Kyriotic Sonship: A Cognitive and Rhetorical Approach to the Characterization of Mark's Jesus*. BIS 148. Leiden: Brill, 2016.

Winn, Adam. *Reading Mark's Christology under Caesar: Jesus the Messiah and the Roman Imperial Ideology*. Downers Grove, IL: InterVarsity, 2018.

4

"DO YOU STILL NOT UNDERSTAND?"

Mark's Disciples

No study of Mark's Gospel would be complete without a discussion of the disciples. The Greek term for "disciples" ($\mu\alpha\theta\eta\tau\alpha\iota$) is used forty-six times in the narrative and typically refers to the twelve individuals called to be "with" Jesus (3:14). Except for ch. 15, the disciples (collectively or individually) appear or are referred to in every chapter of the narrative. And, other than Jesus, no character or character group is mentioned as frequently as the disciples. Their steady presence throughout the narrative is evidence of their literary importance. Indeed, the story of the disciples is intertwined with the story of Jesus and plays a pivotal role in the development of the plot. Through Mark's portrayal of the disciples, the narrator reveals what it means to be a follower of Jesus—one of the main theological themes in the second Gospel.

Telling a complete story of the disciples is beyond the scope of this introductory text. The objective of this chapter is to consider the general depiction of the disciples in Mark's Gospel. The discussion will adopt a thematic approach and will require some movement back and forth across the narrative in order to trace the emerging portrait of the Twelve. It will be shown that Mark's presentation is multifaceted and complex, and perhaps different than often assumed. The portrait oscillates between faith and following to misunderstanding, resistance, and denial, with a notable emphasis on the latter. After considering this variegated and, at times, harsh depiction, the discussion will offer an explanation for Mark's narrative agenda.

FAITH AND FOLLOWING

Discussion of the disciples often focuses on their less than ideal qualities. Though such shortcomings are well attested in the narrative, Mark's portrayal is not one-dimensional. The disciples also display faith and a willingness to follow Jesus. These positive characteristics are sometimes overlooked even though they are exemplified at various places in the narrative.

A Kingdom Call to Repentance and Faith

At face value, Mark 1:14–15 may seem unrelated to the characterization of the disciples. Jesus is the focal point of the scene and the disciples have yet to be introduced into the narrative. Nevertheless, this brief passage has important implications for understanding the portrayal of the disciples in the second Gospel.

Mark 1:14–15 narrates the beginning of Jesus's public ministry in Galilee. Verse 14 offers a temporal description

of Jesus's movements before pivoting to a conceptual summary of his teaching concerning "the gospel of God" (1:14).
After the narrator's description in v. 14, Jesus begins to
speak in the first person, further elaborating on the meaning of the gospel: "The time is fulfilled, and the kingdom of
God has come near; repent, and believe in the good news"
(1:15). Two elements in this statement are noteworthy for
the present discussion. First, the reason for the good news
is that the kingdom of God has been inaugurated. Second,
the announcement of the kingdom is immediately followed
by a command to repent and believe (1:15). Though the
relationship between these elements is not developed, the
close association suggests that the imperatives describe a
proper response to God's activity. That is, repentance and
faith are the means by which an individual enters into God's
kingdom.

But who exactly is one to believe in? Verse 15 refers
to the idea of believing "in the good news," which given
the referent in v. 14 is likely an abbreviated reference to the
"gospel of God." Thus, the announcement of God's kingdom
is designed to inspire faith in God's salvific work. While belief in God seems to be the referent of 1:15, faith in Jesus is
also implied by the near and far context. The same term for
"gospel" is used in the opening verse to summarize the entire narrative: "The beginning of the gospel of Jesus Christ"
(1:1). The overlap between 1:1 and 1:14–15—specifically
the reference to the "gospel" or good news—is suggestive
and underscores Jesus's role in the revelation of God's
"gospel" (1:14). As indicated by his teaching and miraculous deeds, Jesus is the designated herald and authoritative
representative of God's kingdom in Mark's Gospel. The
relationship between the gospel of God and the gospel of
Jesus therefore suggests that faith in God and faith in Jesus
are closely aligned.

Taken together, these two verses have a programmatic function that do more than segue into the body of the narrative. These verses represent a distillation of Jesus's message and have a crucial role in shaping audience perception. The key concepts of 1:14–15 (i.e., kingdom, repentance, faith) are repeated across the narrative (e.g., 1:38, 45; 5:36; 6:12; 8:35; 9:23; 10:29; 11:23; 13:10; 14:9) and simultaneously provide an evaluative standard for the audience to interpret Mark's story. The call to repentance and faith frames how the audience is to assess the responses to Jesus's ministry by the characters in the narrative, including the religious leaders, the various supplicants, and the disciples.

Calling the First Disciples

Immediately after the programmatic statement in 1:14–15, Mark includes two successive scenes that depict the calling of disciples. Mark 1:16–18 describes the call of Simon and Andrew, while 1:19–20 narrates the call of James and John. Both scenes involve two brothers, a fishing context, and an invitation to follow Jesus.

As many scholars have observed, the juxtaposition of 1:14–15 and 1:16–20 is an implicit structural clue that the two units are related. Not only does the sequencing of the material suggest a connection, but the implied imperative "come" in 1:17 (some translations read "follow me") appears to be a synthesis of the double imperative in 1:15 ("repent and believe"). As such, Jesus's actions in the context of Simon and Andrew (1:16–18) and James and John (1:19–20) are an enactment of his kingdom agenda. The language in 1:17 may be different than 1:15, but the call to follow is shorthand for the previous summons to repent and believe.

The disciples' response to Jesus is both terse and revealing. Simon and Andrew leave their fishing net and begin to follow Jesus (1:18). James and John forsake fishing gear, father, and workers to follow Jesus (1:20). This immediate and deliberate action of both parties is a positive sign that indicates a willingness to embrace Jesus's invitation. In the context of 1:14–15, the turning away from one's livelihood exemplifies an idyllic response to God's inbreaking kingdom. Though the account is brief, the actions of Simon/Andrew and James/John embody the initial and programmatic proclamation to repent and believe.

This depiction of the four disciples is intended to be representative of all the disciples (except Judas) and is explicitly evoked later in the narrative. The key scene occurs in Mark 10:28, when Peter affirms that the disciples "have left everything" to follow Jesus (10:28). Peter's statement is made in the first person plural ("we" [10:28]) and suggests that the call narratives (1:14–15, 16–20) are illustrative for all the disciples. In the context of 1:14–20 it seems that the initial depiction of Simon/Andrew and James/John—and thus all the disciples—is undeniably positive. But this interpretation is further suggested by the juxtaposition of Peter's statement in 10:28 with the preceding story of the rich young man (10:17–22), as well as Jesus's teaching on the kingdom of God (10:23–31). Unlike the rich young man who is unwilling to relinquish his earthly possessions and must depart from Jesus in a dejected fashion, the disciples have already acted in a manner that is obedient to Jesus's command. The striking contrast between the rich young man and the disciples indicates that they have already passed through the "eye of the needle" (10:25) and are properly oriented toward the kingdom of God.

The disciples' response, narrated at the beginning of the Gospel and reiterated in 10:28, is indicative of the kind of faith that Mark deems necessary for followers of Jesus. For Mark, discipleship is characterized by a dependency on Jesus and a willingness to embrace the kingdom of God over all allegiances—social, cultural, economic, or political. This totalizing claim (12:29–30) is not merely an act of intellectual ascent but has sweeping consequences. Discipleship involves a complete and ongoing trust that is exemplified by a willingness to forsake all forms of earthly dependency. To this end, the disciples leave their material possessions, their vocations, and their attachments to economic stability, as well as their familial ties, in order to follow Jesus. The disciples become models for all would-be followers by abandoning their unique expressions of human security. Their dependency on God signifies an embrace of God's kingdom and the values of Jesus's inbreaking rule.

Following Jesus

An important scene for appreciating Mark's depiction of the Twelve (or of any character, for that matter) occurs at the midpoint of the narrative as Jesus and the disciples make their way to Caesarea Philippi (8:27–38). After a discussion about his identity, Jesus calls the disciples and crowds to himself. His ensuing statement offers one of the most explicit descriptions about the nature of discipleship in Mark's Gospel:

> [I]f any want to become my followers, let them deny themselves and take up their cross and follow me. For those who want to save their life will lose it, and those who lose their life for my sake, and for the sake of the gospel, will save it. For what will it profit them to gain the whole world and forfeit their life? Indeed, what can they give in return for their life? Those who are ashamed of me and of my words in this adulterous and sinful generation, of them the Son of Man will

    also be ashamed when he comes in the glory of
    his Father with the holy angels. (8:34–38)

This passage is rich with meaning, but there are two important issues that emerge for the present discussion. First, discipleship is costly. Discipleship entails a denial of self and a willingness to identify with Jesus regardless of the consequences. This taking up of the cross involves a readiness to relinquish all for the sake of Jesus. However, any sacrifices that might come as a result of following Jesus are incomparable to the eternal life that awaits those who enter the Father's glory.

Second, for those who are willing to take up their cross, Jesus explicitly invites them to "follow." The Greek term for "follow" is repeated two times in 8:34 and is closely associated with the concept of discipleship in Mark's narrative. Though "following" may have connoted a metaphorical idea for Mark's audience—since, of course, Jesus's earthly ministry was an event in the past—the summons in 8:34–37 has a more literal meaning for the characters in the narrative. In the narrative context, following entailed a physical activity.

These two observations are noteworthy when considering Mark's presentation of the disciples. The call to a life of costly discipleship correlates with the depiction of the Twelve. As has already been observed, the disciples leave their occupations, families, and communities to be with Jesus. By laying aside their earthly allegiances, the disciples have metaphorically taken up their crosses in obedience to Jesus's command. Viewed in this context, the teaching in 8:34–38 offers additional commentary to interpret the actions of the disciples at the beginning of Mark's story.

In addition to their costly actions, Mark describes the disciples as "following" Jesus. In 1:18, Simon and Andrew leave their nets and "follow" Jesus. When Jesus returns to his hometown in 6:1, Mark notes that the disciples "follow" him. Peter, speaking on behalf of the Twelve, reiterates in 10:28 that he and the disciples have left everything to "follow" Jesus. As Jesus makes his way up to Jerusalem, though the narrator does not use the language of following, the concept is nonetheless present as Jesus is described as going before the disciples. Even after the disciples abandon Jesus in the garden, Peter "follows" at a distance into the courtyard of the high priest (14:54). Given the importance of 8:27–33 for understanding Mark's view of discipleship, the language used to describe the disciples cannot be ignored. The terminology is theologically freighted and has positive connotations. Their "following" of Jesus throughout much of the narrative is an interpretive cue that resonates with the standard of discipleship in Mark's Gospel.

Participation in Jesus's Ministry

The positive portrayal of the disciples is further indicated by their active involvement in Jesus's ministry. This is evidenced by their close association with Jesus throughout the narrative and is particularly evident in their commission (3:13–15) and mission (6:7–13, 30), as well as the expectation of their future ministry beyond the resurrection (13:8–13).

The disciples' special relationship to Jesus, suggested by the call narratives (1:16–20), is formalized in their commissioning. In 3:13–15, Jesus goes up on a mountain and "calls" (3:13) a group of individuals to be "with him" (3:14). These twelve individuals, spelled out by name (3:16–19), are designated "apostles" (3:14)[1] and set apart from the other

---

1. The majority of manuscripts do not include the designation "apostles" in Mark 3:14. However, several ancient and significant manuscripts include this reading. See Metzger, *Textual Commentary*, 69.

characters in the narrative. Additional descriptors further link the disciples to the activity of Jesus: the disciples are chosen to "preach" (3:14) and "to have authority to cast out demons" (3:15). The language is suggestive since these activities mirror the deeds of Jesus (1:39; cf. 1:14; 1:23–26, 34). These various points of correspondence heighten the positive connotations associated with the Twelve.

A few chapters after the commission, the disciples are sent out on mission (6:7–13, 30). As before, Jesus "calls" (6:7) the disciples. The Twelve are given "authority" over impure spirits (6:7) and sent forth to "preach" that people might "repent" (6:12). Once again, Mark's depiction is evocative and harkens back to the commissioning (3:13–15). The scene also parallels the narrator's depiction of Jesus in 1:14–15. This paradigmatic scene, which foreshadows Jesus's activities throughout the narrative and is a kind of plot summary, explicitly describes Jesus "preaching" (1:14) and calling people to "repent" (1:15). The deliberate echo bolsters the notion that the disciples' activities are an extension of Jesus's own kingdom work.

As the narrative progresses, the disciples continue to take part in Jesus's ministry. They are with Jesus as he performs mighty deeds and participate in his activities (e.g., 6:31–44; 8:1–9). In addition, ch. 13 describes a scene that projects beyond the narrative and anticipates the disciples' continued ministry after the death of Jesus. The scene is set within an eschatological context and touches on future events, the temple, the return of the Son of Man, and the fall of Jerusalem. Amid the discussion of these issues, Jesus affirms that the disciples will continue to play a vital role in the announcement of God's kingdom. They will "preach" (13:10; cf. 3:14; 6:12) the gospel to the nations and, at great cost, stand before councils, governors, and kings as a witness to Jesus (13:9).

When all of Mark's Gospel is taken into consideration, it must be acknowledged that various texts depict the disciples in a favorable capacity. They respond to Jesus in an exemplary fashion; they are uniquely commissioned to be "with" Jesus; they are attentive to his "calling;" they are sent out in service of his kingdom ministry; and they are envisioned to be unashamed ambassadors after the crucifixion. These unmistakably positive features must be kept in mind as the discussion moves forward and takes a decidedly different direction.

MISUNDERSTANDING, FEAR, AND LACK OF FAITH

The positive portrayal of the disciples is not the only picture that emerges from the second Gospel. Running alongside is a harsh critique that is sustained across a wide swath of the narrative. There are nuances to this depiction that are described in slightly different ways (misunderstanding, fear/lack of faith, hard-heartedness), but the overarching characterization appears to be on a similar trajectory. A brief selection of episodes will demonstrate the pervasiveness and severity of this negative portrayal.

Mark 4:1–32

Through the first three chapters of Mark's Gospel, the characterization of the disciples is entirely positive, save for the reference to Judas Iscariot, whom the narrator observes betrayed Jesus (3:19). The favorable characterization begins to change when Jesus gets into a boat and begins to speak to a large crowd situated on the shore (4:1). Often described as the "parables chapter," the scene begins with a story about a farmer who planted seed on four different soil types (4:1–9). Some of the seed fell along a path and was eaten by birds;

some fell on rocky ground and withered; some fell among the thorns and was choked out; still other seed fell on good soil and produced a bountiful crop.

The explanation of the parable is not given to the crowd but Jesus provides an interpretation for the disciples in 4:14–20, though not before offering a rebuke in 4:13: "Do you not understand this parable? Then how will you understand all the parables?" At first blush, this comment seems entirely unexpected. Why does Jesus respond to the disciples in this fashion? And why should the disciples have understood the parable without an explanation? It is likely that Jesus's response to the disciples stems from the statement in 4:11–12: "To you has been given the secret of the kingdom of God, but for those outside, everything comes in parables; in order that 'they may indeed look, but not perceive, and may indeed listen, but not understand; so that they may not turn again and be forgiven.'"

Though these verses have sparked considerable debate, they appear to affirm that the mysteries of the kingdom have been given to the Twelve. Jesus's handpicked followers are afforded access to know and understand the things of God. If this is the case, Jesus's response in 4:13 seems to fit within the logic of the narrative. Because the disciples have been made insiders, they have been granted insight to decipher the mysteries of God. Yet despite this enablement, they are without understanding and cannot interpret the parable, thus prompting the first of several rebukes in the narrative.

Mark 4:35–41

After a brief summary statement (4:33–34), the critique of the disciples in 4:13 is carried forward into the next episode. There, Jesus departs from the crowds and, along with the disciples, embarks on a sea journey (4:35–36). As the group makes their way across the sea, a fierce storm develops that threatens to capsize the boat. To the shock of the disciples, Jesus is asleep in the stern (4:38) as the waves begin to break over the side of the vessel. Concerned for their welfare, the disciples wake Jesus who then rebukes the wind and waves.

But the scene does not end with Jesus's wonder-working power. After calming the storm, Jesus turns to the disciples: "Why are you afraid? Have you still no faith?" (4:40). The response seems correlated to the previous demonstrations of power that have featured prominently in the narrative (e.g., 1:23–26, 30–31, 32–34, 40–42; 2:1–12; 3:1–5, 10–11). The implication seems to be that if Jesus can heal the sick and cast out demons, then he can be trusted to handle the uncertainties of nautical life. Yet there is a harshness to the rebuke. The second rhetorical question is particularly poignant since it implies not just that the disciples are *lacking* in faith, but that they have "no faith." The sharpness of the response is unmistakable and stands in tension with earlier portions of the narrative (see the discussion above) that portray the disciples as exemplars of faith. The resulting depiction is so troubling that Matthew changes Mark's "no faith" to "little faith" (Matt 8:26), thereby softening the characterization of the Twelve.

Mark 6:7–30

It has already been observed that the disciples are commissioned by Jesus in 3:13–15 and sent on mission in 6:7–13, 30. Because their actions parallel the deeds of Jesus, the depiction is infused—seemingly—with a positive nuance. However, the episode is complexified by the wider narrative context.

Mark's arrangement of the journey is interesting, for as soon as the disciples depart (6:12–13), the narrative immediately shifts to the story of John the Baptist (6:14–29). The scene describes John's arrest, imprisonment, and the banquet that eventually leads to his beheading. After John's story is told the narrative returns to the disciples' regathering (6:30). One could argue that the arrangement is designed to provide a historical interlude for the sending and return of the disciples. But it is noteworthy that the placement of John's death is not for chronological purposes. The scene is a flashback (6:17) that narrates what has occurred at an earlier point in the narrative. The events could have been inserted elsewhere, but Mark has deliberately placed the scene within the context of the disciples' mission. But why? What purpose does this serve in Mark's story?

The sequence of events in 6:7–30 is structured as a Markan sandwich (see ch. 2). The intercalation of scenes, so common in Mark, is a deliberate rhetorical device that is designed to invite audience reflection and participation. To appreciate how and why the scenes are related, it may be helpful to consider the final verse in the sequence. When the disciples regather around Jesus, Mark indicates that the disciples "told him all they had done and taught" (6:30). What is noticeably absent in this statement is any affirmation that the power and authority experienced by the disciples is at all dependent on Jesus (3:14–15; 6:7). This subtle omission suggests an important misunderstanding and a preoccupation with the disciples' own achievements.

This perspective stands in stark relief to the depiction of John the Baptist, whose story is sandwiched between the disciples' sending and return. The juxtaposition of these episodes underscores the contrasting perspectives. Like the disciples, John is also called and sent on a mission (1:2–4). Although he is unjustly imprisoned and suffers a cruel death that is set in motion by a rash vow, the narrative indicates that he continued to be a righteous and holy man (6:20) who proclaimed a message of repentance for the forgiveness of sins (1:4; 6:20). The boldness of his faith and obedience, culminating in his unjust death, is a model of discipleship (cf. 8:34) that prefigures the death of Jesus.

The sandwiching of John's story with the disciples' is a deliberate narrative device that accentuates the contrast between characters. Although John's story concludes with his tragic demise, while the disciples' ends on a note of outward success, the audience recognizes that there is a profound irony at play. The disciples' confusion and self-aggrandizement stand in sharp distinction from the exemplary depiction of John. As the narrative continues to advance, there is a growing suspicion that the Twelve do not fully understand their calling, who Jesus is (4:3–41), or what it means to be a disciple (6:7–30).

Mark 6:33–44

The disciples' enjoyment of their missionary "success" is carried forward into the next scene. After returning from their journey, Jesus attempts to withdraw with the disciples to a lonely place in order to rest (6:31–32). As the group enters a boat, Mark states that the people "saw *them*" and raced ahead on foot to a designated location (6:33). Previous to this episode, the crowds had always been drawn to *Jesus* (cf. 1:45; 2:13; 3:8; 4:1). But now they identify Jesus *and* the disciples, further underscoring the notoriety of the Twelve.

This elevation in public status does not seem to correspond with any growth in understanding. When the boat arrives at shore, Jesus is met by a great multitude who are "like sheep without a shepherd" (6:34). As Jesus begins to teach "many things" (6:34), the disciples take stock of the situation and express concern for the welfare of the people. Noting the late hour and the remote location, the disciples instruct (with an imperative) Jesus to send the crowd away in order that they might buy something to eat (6:35). Jesus responds, however, with an imperative of his own commanding the disciples to "give them something to eat" (6:37).

The disciples' response to Jesus is telling and further reveals their lack of insight. The disciples rightly point out that to feed such a crowd would require tremendous resources (two hundred denarii [6:37]). In a context where a denarius was equivalent to a day's wage (cf. Matt 20:2), Jesus's command seems unrealistic and imprudent. But the disciples' response appears to ignore what Jesus has already accomplished and what the disciples have already experienced. Not only have the disciples been spectators to Jesus's wonder-working activities, but they too have participated in this kingdom power—in the preceding episode! If Jesus can exert authority over nature, demons, disease, and death itself (4:35–43), surely he can provide for a crowd in a desolate location.

But there is an even deeper irony in the disciples' response. When Jesus asks about their provisions, the disciples confess to having "five [loaves] and two fish" (6:38). The admission is telling for the disciples were previously instructed to take no bread on their journey (6:8). The disciples have now acquired bread and seemingly forgotten about God's provision through their ministry. Once again, Jesus will meet the needs of the people by multiplying the loaves and fishes. However, the disciples' response to the situation demonstrates profound confusion.

Mark 8:22—10:52

The final passage exemplifying the disciples' incomprehension is not a single episode but a segment of material that spans two chapters. The unit is demarcated by the healing of two blind men. The first comes in the region of Bethsaida (8:22–26) and the second as Jesus is leaving Jericho on his way to Jerusalem (10:46–52). Between the episodes are various other scenes. However, the healing of the blind men appears to be framed around three passion predictions (8:31–33; 9:31–32; 10:32–34). The connection between these events is directly related to the characterization of the Markan disciples.

The sequence of events begins in Bethsaida when a blind man is brought to Jesus for healing. Events of this kind are a mainstay of the narrative, and the audience has been well prepared for this type of scene. In such contexts, a supplicant approaches or is brought to Jesus for healing; the individual is restored by Jesus's word or touch; and finally, the individual is sent away and/or Jesus departs. The scene in Bethsaida, however, is unique. After Jesus leads the man outside the village, he spits on his eyes and lays his hands on him (8:23). He then asks, "Can you see anything?" (8:23) to which the man replies, "I can see people, but they look like trees, walking" (8:24). The response causes Jesus to touch the man a second time in order to bring full restoration. What makes the scene so unique is that it appears to take two attempts to heal the man. The depiction is so startling that none of the other Gospels include this episode, presumably for theological reasons (could Jesus not heal the man on the first try?). This feature of the narrative only adds intrigue and begs for an explanation.

In order to address this issue, it is necessary to turn to Jesus's threefold passion prediction. Though there is slight variation among the accounts, the predictions follow a similar pattern. In each, Jesus instructs his disciples about the events that are to unfold in Jerusalem. In no uncertain terms, Jesus tells the disciples that he, the Son of Man, will be rejected and killed, and after three days rise from the dead. The repetition not only foreshadows the remainder of the narrative but also links the sequence of events in Mark 8:22—10:45.

The repetition of the threefold passion prediction is likewise followed by another kind of repetition, albeit in the form of the disciples' response. After the first passion prediction (8:31–33), Peter openly rebukes Jesus (8:32). Peter (speaking on behalf of the disciples) cannot fathom how the Messiah must suffer and die. His response to Jesus indicates that Peter has not come to grips with the full scope of Jesus's mission.

The second passion prediction (9:31–32) develops in a similar manner. As Jesus and the disciples make their way through Galilee, Jesus again informs the disciples that he will be delivered into the hands of men, killed, and three days later rise from the dead. Unlike the first prediction, there is no confrontation between Jesus and the disciples. However, the narrator succinctly notes that "the disciples did not understand what he was saying and were afraid to ask him" (9:32).

The final passion prediction (10:32–34) follows the same path as the previous two. The revelation of Jesus does as much to expose the disciples' confusion as it does to foreshadow the cross. Unlike the previous predictions, the disciples do not offer an immediate response to Jesus nor does the narrator provide an assessment of their mental state. The disciples' lack of understanding—so evident in the previous predictions—is exemplified in the immediately following scene.

In Mark 10:35–44, James and John approach Jesus and ask him "to do for us whatever we ask" (10:35). Jesus responds to the disciples by asking a question of his own: "What is it you want me to do for you?" (10:36). The disciples reply by requesting to sit at Jesus's right and left when he enters his "glory" (10:37). It is not entirely clear whether this glory refers to some type of eschatological reign or an earthly kingdom that the disciples assume will be established by Jesus. What does seem evident is that the petition is a plea for power as the imagery conjures up depictions of exaltation and co-enthronement (e.g., Ps 110 or Dan 7).

This brash and bold request is an explicit indication of the disciples' underlying motivation and a further demonstration of their skewed perspective. The disciples remain concerned with their own status and power, having gleaned something about Jesus's coming glory (8:38) but nothing about his service and sacrifice. Jesus goes on to question James and John about their request, suggesting that they too will share in his suffering. Yet the most succinct and poignant assessment of the disciples comes from Jesus himself: "You do not know what you are asking" (10:38).

The episode is also noteworthy because it is located immediately before the final scene of the sequence, the healing of blind Bartimaeus (10:46–52). As Bartimaeus is sitting by the roadside, he is told that Jesus is passing by and begins to cry out, "Jesus, Son of David, have mercy on me!" (10:47). Though discouraged by others, Bartimaeus is unpersuaded and continues to make his plea (10:48). Eventually, Jesus hears Bartimaeus and calls for him (10:49). Jesus then asks Bartimaeus a question: "What do you want me to do for you?" (10:51). After Bartimaeus petitions to have his vision restored, the scene concludes with his healing and the commendation of his faith (10:52).

The discerning interpreter will recognize a striking similarity between the story of James and John and the story of blind Bartimaeus. In both accounts, Jesus asks virtually the exact same question: "What do you want me to do for you?" (10:36, 51). The deliberate repetition is an explicit clue that the two scenes are connected. Though the relationship is not drawn out in any detail, Mark structures the narrative to invite a deeper level of reflection. The scenes encourage the audience to consider Jesus's question in relation to the two responses.

When Jesus queries James and John, they reply by asking for positions of power (10:37). Although they seemingly ask under the pretense of sitting in Jesus's "glory," there is little doubt that they are concerned with their own self-interest. Bartimaeus, in contrast, appears for only a brief moment in the narrative. He is troubled by a physical ailment that has left him destitute and begging on the roadside. With no hint of an ulterior motive, Bartimaeus asks only to regain his sight. Jesus not only grants the request but commends Bartimaeus's demonstrable faith (10:52). The two responses to Jesus are diametrically opposed. One is governed by self-interest, while the other stems from a genuine desire for restoration. One reflects a deep misunderstanding, while the other is infused with an insight that more than compensates for the lack of eyesight.

When all of the pieces from 8:22—10:52 are considered, it appears that a primary point of emphasis is the disciples' continued confusion and inadequacy. They are still without understanding. Three times Jesus explicitly instructs the disciples about the events that await him in Jerusalem. In each instance, the disciples respond in a fashion that further demonstrates their own self-interest. They simply cannot come to terms with the cross and, relatedly, what it means to be a follower of this suffering Messiah.

In narrative terms, they are blind—unable to understand what has been communicated to them on three separate occasions. Like the blind man in Bethsaida, the disciples have received a proverbial first touch, but their response to Jesus indicates that they too do not have clarity of vision. Of course, there is hope that the disciples can and perhaps will begin to see clearly. But with each successive passion prediction the disciples continue to evidence greater confusion. The cycle comes to a dramatic conclusion with the story of James and John who reveal themselves to be partially blind and still in need of a second restorative touch.

If faith and following demarcate the initial portrayal of the disciples, misunderstanding, fear, and a lack of faith begin to appear shortly thereafter. Though it is true that the disciples continue to follow after Jesus, there has been a discernible shift in the characterization of the Twelve. Ironically, those who are closest to Jesus seem most confused about what it means to be a follower of Jesus.

RESISTANCE TO JESUS'S MISSION

There are numerous instances in the narrative where the disciples display a somewhat benign ineptitude. But there are other occasions where their misunderstanding leads to expressions of active and passive resistance. Take, for example, Peter's so-called confession and response to the first passion prediction in 8:27–33. Peter's reaction is jolting and demonstrates a palpable level of confusion, particularly since the rebuke employs language that was previously used in the exorcism of demons (1:25; 3:12). Yet Jesus's response is even more shocking as he identifies Peter *as Satan* ("Get behind me, Satan!" [8:33]). Whatever might be said about this exchange, at least for the moment, it appears that the disciples have slipped from being "with" Jesus (3:14) to against Jesus. The shift from misunderstanding to resistance is identifiable in several additional scenes, which are clustered around Mark's gentile mission and a sequence of events that revolve around the motif of bread.

Mark 6:33–44

Jesus's first bread miracle has already been discussed above. Though the basic outline of the story is easily comprehensible, there are a few details that should be unpacked in order to appreciate how the scene functions in the broader narrative. In particular, several elements suggest that the scene is cast in a Jewish setting. There are a number of allusions to the Jewish Scriptures, including the desert setting (6:31–32, 35), the association of Jesus as shepherd (6:34), and the people being instructed to sit in companies of hundreds and fifties (6:39–40)—all of which are tied in some form to Israel's exodus experience (Exod 18:21–25; Num 27:17; 31:14; Deut 1:15). In addition, it is not coincidental that the people are told by the shepherd (Jesus) to recline on green grass (6:34, 39)—an allusion to imagery in Ps 23—and that there are twelve baskets of leftovers (6:43)—symbolizing the twelve tribes of Israel. These seemingly insignificant details paint a thoroughly Jewish backdrop for Jesus's first bread miracle. Though the details appear trivial, the Jewish setting will become highly significant as the narrative progresses.

Mark 6:45–53

Immediately after the first bread miracle, Jesus directs the disciples to go ahead of him to Bethsaida. As the disciples attempt to reach Bethsaida via the sea, Jesus heads up a mountain to pray. During the early morning, while it is still dark and the disciples are struggling to make headway, Jesus approaches the disciples on the water. Frightened by the appearance of a water-walking Jesus, the disciples cry out in fear at this unusual sight. Jesus identifies himself, gets into the boat, and the sea becomes still.

Even a cursory reading of the passage suggests that the disciples are without understanding. Mark indicates that the disciples are fearful and astonished (6:49, 51) and explicitly states that "they did not understand" (6:52). The disciples' failure to even recognize Jesus is all the more pronounced in light of the subtle intertextual echoes that collectively point to his true identity (see ch. 3). In a moment when Jesus should be most understood (that is, when he is doing the kinds of things that only God can do), the disciples are once again confused and bewildered. At the very least, the mistaking of Jesus for a ghost is all the more bizarre since ancient people did not believe that ghosts could walk on water.[2]

The disciples' confusion is relatively obvious, but there is more at stake than a simple case of misunderstanding. This is now the second instance where the disciples have experienced some form of struggle on the sea (4:35–41; 6:45–53). There have been four sea crossings thus far (4:35–41; 5:21; 6:32–34, 45–53). Two are narrated without incident (5:21; 6:32–34) and two involve some form of conflict (4:35–41; 6:45–53). It seems significant that there is turmoil only when the disciples are travelling from west to east or into gentile territory. When the disciples travel to Jewish territory (east to west), the sea is presumably calm and requires nothing more than a quick summary statement.

What is even more unusual about 6:45–53 is that the disciples are instructed to go to Bethsaida (gentile territory).

2. Combs, "Ghost on the Water?"

However, when the group finally arrives, they land at Gennesaret, on the western Jewish side of the sea (6:53). One could assume that the boat was blown off course, but this is nowhere indicated in the text. The landing spot is all the more unusual since the disciples had previously experienced a more daunting storm yet somehow arrived at their intended destination (4:35–41). That Simon, Andrew, James, and John are described as experienced fishermen (1:16, 19) makes this feature all the more intriguing.

What explains this narrative anomaly? It may be that the depiction is symbolic. That is, the disciples' "struggle" on the sea may be suggestive of their subtle resistance to the gentile mission. Though Jesus has already received gentiles (3:8) and crossed over into gentile territory (5:1–20), the disciples "straining at the oars" (6:48) may imply more than a physical inability. It is significant that the scene begins with Jesus having to "compel" the disciples into the boat (6:45) and concludes with the note that their "hearts were hardened"—a poignant phrase that looks back to the Exodus and Pharaoh's *resistance* to God's initiative (Exod 7:13–14, 22; 8:15, 19, 32; 9:7, 12, 34–35; 10:1, 20, 27; 11:10; 14:8).[3] This theme will continue to develop, but there is some basis to suggest that the disciples are not only ignorant of Jesus's mission, but resistant to the extension of God's kingdom beyond the Jewish homeland.

Mark 7:1—8:9

Jesus and the disciples will eventually make their way to Bethsaida (8:22), but not before an interlude in the narrative. The sequence of episodes in Mark 7:1–30 may appear

---

3. Whether God or the disciples is the initiator of the hardening is not entirely clear in Mark. In either case, it appears that the disciples, like Pharaoh, are willing participants in the hardening.

unrelated to the theme of gentile inclusion, but they are intricately tied to Mark's theological agenda. Indeed, the repeated mention of "bread" is a narrative clue that the episodes are thematically related.

Chapter 7 begins with a controversy between Jesus and the religious establishment. In 7:1–13, Jesus is questioned by the scribes and Pharisees about matters of ritual purity. When the disciples are observed eating "bread" with unwashed hands (7:2), Jesus is asked why his disciples do not observe the tradition of the elders (7:5). After a narrative aside explaining some of the ritualistic practices followed by "all" Jews (7:3–4), Jesus goes on to expose the hypocrisy of the religious leaders. The scene closes with the Markan Jesus insisting that the Jewish leaders have nullified "the word of God" and that they do "many things like this" (7:13).

The ensuing episode follows hard on the heels of Jesus's confrontation with the religious establishment and returns to the theme of food (7:14–23). However, whereas the response in 7:1–13 focuses on why the disciples do not live according to the tradition of the elders, vv. 14–23 offer a direct answer to the original question posed by the religious leaders. Calling the crowd to himself, Jesus declares that "nothing outside a person . . . by going in can defile" (7:15). What defiles a person are the things that "come out" of the body (7:15). Without further explanation, Jesus and the disciples leave the crowd and enter into a home where the disciples begin to question Jesus about the "parable" (7:17). Once again, the disciples are without understanding (7:18) and in need of a fuller explanation.

> "Do you not see that whatever goes into a person from outside cannot defile, since it enters, not the heart but the stomach, and goes out into the sewer?" (Thus he declared all foods clean.) And

> he said, "It is what comes out of a person that
> defiles. For it is from within, from the human
> heart, that evil intentions come: fornication,
> theft, murder, adultery, avarice, wickedness,
> deceit, licentiousness, envy, slander, pride, folly.
> All these evil things come from within, and they
> defile a person." (7:18–23)

In this brief but arresting statement, Mark's Jesus overturns the Jewish food laws. Impurity is a condition of the heart that originates from within and manifests itself in outward expressions of ungodliness. Food does not make a person unclean. The further implication seems to be that, just as food cannot defile, neither can an object or person contaminate through any form of physical contact.

Immediately after Jesus's statement on impurity, Jesus and the disciples travel to the gentile region of Tyre (7:24–30). While in a home, Jesus is confronted by an unnamed woman whose daughter is demon possessed. Mark notes that the woman is a "Gentile, of Syrophoenician origin" (7:26) who comes on behalf of her demon-possessed daughter. The response between Jesus and the woman is worth quoting in full:

> And he [Jesus] said to her, "Let the children be
> satisfied first, for it is not right to take the children's bread and throw it to the dogs." But she
> answered and said to him, "Lord, even the dogs
> under the table eat the children's crumbs." And
> he said to her, "Because of this word, go! The
> demon has left your daughter." (7:27–29)[4]

There are three items of note in this exchange. First, the subject of bread is once more put forth in the narrative (7:27–28). At this point, it is not mere happenstance. The

---

4. My own translation.

repeated use of the motif suggests a deliberate narrative design.

Second, the discussion between Jesus and the woman involves the use of parabolic language (children, bread, dogs). The manner of expression is indirect, cryptic, and requires some interpretation (for the characters and the audience). Recall Jesus's earlier statement that parables are designed to obscure as much as they are to reveal: "For those outside, everything comes in parables; in order that 'they may indeed look, but not perceive, and may indeed listen, but not understand'" (4:11–12). It is quite unexpected then that the Syrophoenician woman requires no explanation. Although the disciples must inquire about a comparatively simple parable in the proceeding episode (7:17–23), an unnamed woman is able to enter into a parabolic dialogue with the Markan Jesus. She comprehends the parable and extends the discussion using the same symbolic language without any hesitation (7:28).

Third, if the parabolic elements represent Israel (children), the blessings associated with God's kingdom (bread), and the gentiles (dogs), then Jesus appears to rebuff the woman's request (7:27). His response seems to affirm that God's blessings (in this case, the gift of healing) are reserved first for the Jewish people. Since the woman is a gentile, her request is an infringement on the children's "bread." But if this common interpretation is correct, it is at odds with a narrative that describes Jesus as already welcoming gentiles (3:7–12). Moreover, Jesus has already initiated a journey into gentile territory and healed a man with a legion of demons (5:1–20). To suggest that Jesus tersely rejects the woman's request disrupts the logic of the narrative. It would appear that the narrative has been steadily advancing toward the full inclusion of gentiles.

To understand Jesus's response, it is imperative to situate the episode within the broader development of the bread sequence (Mark 6–8). The affirmation that the children are "to be satisfied" first (7:27) recalls that the Jewish people have already been "satisfied" (6:42) in the multiplication of loaves and fishes (6:33–44). Indeed, they were "satisfied" to such an extent that there was an overabundance of provisions (6:43). The narrative then moves quickly to the disciples' eating (bread) with unwashed hands (7:1–30). The scene provides an opportunity to clarify that being "unclean" is not determined by the consumption of certain foods or adhering to ritualistic practices or even ethnic identity. What makes a person unclean are the things that originate from within. An individual's standing before God is ultimately determined by the purity of their heart.

This deliberate arrangement of the narrative—the focus on Jesus's acceptance of gentiles and the abolishment of the food laws—must be considered when interpreting Jesus's response to the Syrophoenician woman in 7:27. The blessings of the kingdom have already been extended to the gentiles and the Jewish people have already "been satisfied." In view of these narrative developments, Jesus's response to the Syrophoenician woman is best understood as an implicit test—a kind of verbal challenge to deduce the genuineness of her intentions. That the woman is able to understand Jesus's parabolic statement and respond in a theologically informed fashion reveals not only her faith, but also—in view of the wider context—the condition of her heart. In conformity with the new standards of purity explicated by Mark's Jesus, the Syrophoenician woman, although a gentile, demonstrates that she too is pure in heart and acceptable to God.

After healing a deaf, gentile man in the region of the Decapolis (7:31–37)—further indicating that the "dogs under the table" (7:28) have ears to hear—the "bread" sequence comes to a close in 8:1–9. Again, Jesus feeds a large crowd by multiplying loaves and fishes, leaving the crowd "satisfied" (8:8). The scene is so strikingly similar to the feeding in 6:33–44 that some have suggested the two accounts are variants of a single pre-Markan tradition. Yet regardless of the origins, the two bread miracles are to be distinguished in the narrative. The first multiplication of loaves occurs in Jewish territory, while the second takes place in gentile territory. The various OT allusions that were subtly woven into the first feeding are absent in the second. Even the term that identifies the "baskets" used to collect leftovers is deliberately altered. While on Jewish soil the disciples make use of a distinct wicker basket (6:43) that "every Jew carried" (Juvenal, *Sat.* 3.14; 6.542). In gentile territory, Mark uses a different, more generic term. That the disciples collect twelve baskets of pieces in Jewish territory (6:43)—symbolizing the twelve tribes of Israel—and seven baskets in gentile territory (8:8)—referring to the seventy nations of the world (Gen 10:2–31)—is a carefully placed detail to differentiate between the episodes.

The scene vividly illustrates that both Jews and gentiles are acceptable to God and that the blessings of the kingdom are sufficient for *all* people. Though there is a theology of inclusion at play in the narrative, there is likewise a countermovement, evidenced by the disciples' divergent responses. Among the Jewish people, the disciples, like Jesus (6:34), demonstrate compassion by encouraging Jesus to send the crowd away to secure necessary provisions (6:35–36). But when the disciples find themselves in a different but more uncertain situation among gentiles (i.e., the crowd had been with Jesus for three days [8:2]), they make no attempt to intervene on behalf of the people to ensure their well-being. Their indifference is all the more striking since Jesus's teaching and actions testify to his genuine love for all people.

Mark 8:13–22

The disciples' response to the gentile mission takes its most dramatic step in the third and final sea crossing (8:13–22). Once again, Jesus and the disciples enter a boat and attempt to cross over into gentile Bethsaida. The alert audience member will recall that Bethsaida was previously mentioned in 6:45–53. In that scene, Jesus and the disciples set off for Bethsaida but strangely come to shore on the Jewish side of the sea. Much has transpired in the narrative since then to underscore the universal scope of Jesus's mission. Jesus has paved the way for gentile inclusion by abolishing the food laws (7:1–23), demonstrating that gentiles can be "clean" (7:24–30), and extending the blessings of God's kingdom to those outside Israel (8:1–9). Given this narrative instruction, the question remains whether the disciples have gained any insight from the loaves or whether they are still without understanding (6:52) as they make their way to gentile Bethsaida.

Similar to the first two sea crossings (4:35–41; 6:45–53), the third also involves conflict. Unlike the previous journeys in which the disciples faced opposition from the forces of nature, the third journey features relational conflict between Jesus and the disciples. As has been the case throughout 6:33—8:22 (with the exception of 7:31–37), a reference to bread becomes a focal point of the narrative, thus linking the entire sequence of events and the underlying issue of gentile inclusion. The conflict arises on the curious note that—except for a single loaf—the disciples had "forgotten" to take bread on their journey (8:14). Jesus then begins to instruct the disciples about "the yeast of the

Pharisees and the yeast of Herod" (8:15), of which the disciples mistakenly assume that the saying has to do with their lack of provisions. The comical misunderstanding prompts Jesus to issue a series of poignant questions: "Why are you talking about having no bread? Do you still not perceive or understand? Are your hearts hardened? Having eyes do you not see, and having ears do you not hear?" (8:17–18). Though the barrage of questions spotlights the disciples' misunderstanding and resistance, what specifically have the disciples been hardened to?

Central to appreciating the exchange is recognizing that the term "forgotten" (8:14) may not provide an adequate translation of the underlying Greek. The term occurs only 7 times in the NT but some 122 times in the LXX (the Greek translation of the OT). In the overwhelming number of cases in the LXX, the term does not refer to an accidental or inadvertent lapse in memory. Instead, the term means to "overlook consciously" or "to neglect willfully" and is frequently used in contexts describing Israel's covenantal unfaithfulness.[5] This use of the term is illustrated, for example, in Jer 18:15: "[M]y people have forgotten me, they burn incense to false gods." The author is not suggesting that the people have carelessly or haphazardly "forgotten" to worship God. Just the opposite. The people have deliberately and intentionally turned away from God. Their "forgetting" is a willful act.

In view of this lexical context, the interpreter should not assume that the disciples have inadvertently forgotten to bring provisions when setting out for gentile Bethsaida. Their actions represent a conscious and willful decision. When set within the larger narrative frame, their choice of provisioning takes on an even more sinister nuance. In view of Jesus's ongoing mission to the gentiles, the failed

5. Gibson, "Rebuke of the Disciples."

trip to Bethsaida, and the ongoing instruction about the inclusiveness of God's kingdom, it appears that the disciples have *chosen* to bring a single loaf of bread. Why? So that the resources can be expended on their own needs rather than the gentiles'. This conscious act of disobedience is subtle, but expresses a form of defiance that is targeted at Jesus's inclusive mission to the gentiles. Such a response explains why for the second time in the narrative the disciples are described as having hardened hearts (8:17; cf. 6:52). This unflattering depiction of the Twelve reaches a crescendo in Mark's passion narrative.

THE DENIAL OF JESUS

From relatively early on in the narrative there are clues that Jesus will be "taken away" (2:20). Though the details surrounding his death remain vague, the audience knows that the religious leaders (3:6) and Judas (3:19) will play a role. What remains to be seen is how the disciples respond to Jesus's arrest, trial, and crucifixion. A brief and selective analysis will show that although Mark's depiction is decidedly negative, the narrative reintegrates the spectrum of traits—faith, misunderstanding, and resistance—from the whole of the narrative.

It is often observed that Mark's Gethsemane account, when Jesus agonizes over his impending death (14:32–42), points forward to the crucifixion; however, it is equally important to note that the episode looks backwards as well. The scene in the garden is closely linked to Mark 13 via a catchword that is variously translated "to keep watch," "to stay awake," or "to stay alert." The term occurs three times in Mark 13 (vv. 34, 35, 37) and three times in Mark 14 (vv. 34, 37, 38). As is often the case, the deliberate repetition is a structural device signaling a narrative connection.

The scene in Gethsemane follows Mark's often-used pattern of three. On three occasions, Jesus leaves the disciples to pray—repeatedly telling them to "keep watch." After each instance Jesus returns to find the disciples sleeping (14:37, 40, 41). It hardly needs mentioning that the disciples' actions are not a reflection of their confident trust in God (cf. 4:35–41). Despite having been warned to "keep watch" (13:34, 35, 37) lest they be caught unprepared, the disciples are found "sleeping" (14:36) in Jesus's hour of need. The explicit disobedience to the command portrays the disciples in a negative fashion and further demonstrates that they have little understanding or situational awareness. The disciples are oblivious to the unfolding events—even though they had been explicitly instructed about Jesus's impending passion (8:31; 9:31; 10:32–34).

The link between Mark 13 and 14 accentuates the negative depiction of the disciples, but it also points in a surprisingly different direction as well. Amid the various commands in Mark 13 to "keep watch" (13: 34, 35, 37) and to "beware" (13:2, 5, 9, 23, 33), the discourse also describes the future endeavors of the disciples. Because of their relationship to Jesus, the disciples will be delivered to the courts and flogged in synagogues (13:9). They will stand before governmental officials and, by the power of the Spirit, they will confidently give testimony for the sake of the gospel (13:9–11). They will experience relational struggle and will be "hated by all" because of their fidelity to Jesus (13:13). Though this portrait of the disciples—committed, confident, and willing to suffer—may seem at odds with a scene in which they are unable to stay awake, Mark deliberately holds these depictions in tension. Their future ministerial activity (cf. 14:27–28) counterbalances the disappointment of Gethsemane as the two chapters intersperse both positive and negative portrayals of the disciples.

The subsequent arrest of Jesus, in the scene immediately after Gethsemane, is entirely negative (14:43–52). Not only is one of the disciples, Judas, the betrayer of Jesus, but the disciples' actions during the arrest are equally as troubling. When Jesus is seized by the arresting party, "one of those who stood near drew his sword and struck the slave of the high priest, cutting off his ear" (14:47). Mark does not identify who performed this act. Some have suggested that it was a bystander who intervened on behalf of Jesus. But there is no contextual evidence to suggest that someone other than a disciple is responsible for the action (cf. Matt 26:52; Luke 22:49–50; John 18:10). One might be inclined to interpret this as an indication of the disciples' loyalty to Jesus. However, given the threefold passion prediction and the direct affirmation that these events are in accord with God's will (14:49), the response of the anonymous disciple has a negative connotation. Indeed, the act is similar to Peter's demonically inspired rebuke of Jesus earlier in the narrative (8:31–33). Though the anonymous disciple appears to act for Jesus, like Peter, he too has resisted the will of God and has set his mind "on human things" (8:33).

The characterization of the disciples only spirals downward from here. In a succinct and revealing statement the narrator concludes, "All of them deserted him and fled" (14:50). Mark's assessment of this desertion is symbolically portrayed in the subsequent depiction of a young man who was "following" Jesus (like the disciples), is caught up in the arrest, and is forced to flee naked (14:51–52). Though a strange scene that is not repeated in the other Gospels, the close association between the disciples and the young man is typically regarded as the narrator's unflattering portrayal of the Twelve. The young man may have escaped, but a cloud of shame overshadows his actions (like the disciples).

Despite the fact that the narrative describes the flight of "all" the disciples (14:50), Peter follows Jesus "at a distance" (14:54) into the courtyard of the high priest. His unwillingness to fully embrace Jesus, already indicated in v. 50 and v. 54, is writ large in the ensuing trial scene. There, as accusations are leveled against Jesus and he is convicted of blasphemy, Peter is confronted by servant girls and bystanders about his relationship to Jesus (14:66–72).

The scene of Peter's denial unfolds in a pattern of three. In the first iteration of the sequence, a servant girl addresses Peter: "You also were with Jesus, the man from Nazareth" (14:67). The statement is immediately rebuffed by Peter, who responds by seemingly playing dumb: "I do not know or understand what you are talking about" (14:68). Of course, the audience recognizes the irony. The disciples have been without understanding throughout much of the narrative. The second encounter, though brief, evidences slight development as Peter denies being "one of them" (14:69). In the climactic third scene as Peter is addressed by the bystanders, he goes so far as to disavow any relationship to or knowledge about Jesus, swearing in oath: "I do not know this man you are talking about" (14:71).

With these words the story of the disciples comes to a dramatic conclusion. A story that begins with promise and hope culminates on a note of denial and abandonment. Though the disciples vow to die with Jesus rather than deny him (14:31), they have forsaken their commitment. Instead, they desert Jesus rather than expose themselves to a fateful death with him. Peter's tragic rejection is the final appearance by one of the Twelve in Mark's Gospel.

Conclusion

Mark's characterization of the disciples is unflattering, harsh, and direct. The disciples are fearful, dim-witted, confused, obtuse, and, at times, opposed to God's will. But Mark's characterization is not one-dimensional. The disciples forsake family and livelihoods to follow Jesus, and they are described as becoming unashamed ambassadors of Jesus after the resurrection. When the entirety of the narrative is considered, Mark's portrait of the disciples is complex and multifaceted. Exactly how the interpreter is to account for this characterization is the subject of the final section.

ASSESSMENT OF THE DISCIPLES' CHARACTERIZATION

We began the chapter by observing that the depiction of the disciples is a vehicle by which the theme of discipleship is articulated in the narrative. The assumption behind this assertion is that the second Gospel is more than a historical account aimed to provide data about the person of Jesus. Instead, it is written with the audience in mind to challenge, inform, and encourage would-be followers of Jesus. Because discipleship is interconnected with Mark's disciples, the only outstanding question is how the audience is to assess the characterization of the Twelve. More specifically, how is the audience to evaluate Mark's disciples in view of the totality of the narrative? And why is Mark's depiction of the disciples so harsh? Though a response to this question has already been alluded to, for the sake of clarity it will be helpful to consider two different approaches that have been adopted in the history of Markan scholarship.

Disassociation/Rejection

For many scholars, there can be no relieving Mark's negative depiction. The disciples do embody Jesus's message at the beginning of the narrative: they serve as models of faith and quickly follow after Jesus. But these admirable traits are soon minimized in the central section of the narrative, where the disciples are repeatedly and consistently portrayed as without faith and understanding. As the narrative progresses, the depiction of the Twelve continues to spiral downward and ultimately comes to a "disastrous conclusion" as the disciples abandon and deny Jesus altogether.[6] What begins in a positive manner concludes in such a catastrophic fashion that it overshadows the overall characterization of the disciples.

It has often been argued that this thoroughgoing and negative depiction is intended to lead to a complete rejection of the disciples. Because of the portrayal, the audience is left with no alternative but to distance themselves from those who are closest to Jesus. As a testament to the severity of the depiction, this disassociation or rejection has been advocated by scholars adopting various hermeneutical perspectives. Some, for example, have offered a historical rationale, suggesting that the polemic against the disciples is intended to discredit a conservative Jerusalem church (represented by the disciples)[7] or a faulty Christology that was advancing in the Markan community (and associated with the disciples).[8] Others utilizing a literary approach have come to a similar conclusion based on the trajectory of the narrative.[9] Regardless of the particulars, both perspectives

---

6. Tannehill, "Disciples in Mark," 403.

7. Tyson, "Blindness of the Disciples"; Kelber, *Kingdom in Mark*.

8. Weeden, *Mark*.

9. Williams, *Other Followers of Jesus*.

maintain that the depiction creates an irreconcilable divide between the disciples and the audience. These interpretations will be explored in greater detail in the discussion of Mark's ending (see ch. 6). For now, it is sufficient to observe that because of the narrative plotting, some argue that the audience is left with no alternative but to disassociate from the disciples either within or beyond the narrative.

Association/Identification

While it is difficult to deny the severity of Mark's depiction, others have argued that the portrayal is not intended to spur rejection, but rather identification with the disciples. Though these interpretations are diametrically opposed, there are at least three reasons for affirming this latter approach.

First, as previously observed, the narrative depiction of the disciples begins on an affirming note. On this point, there is no disagreement. At issue is the function of the introductory portrayal in view of the broader narrative. For those arguing that the disciples are to be rejected, the first several chapters only accentuate the disciples' fall from grace. But it is also possible that the initial characterization lays the groundwork for the audience and is the lens by which to interpret the remainder of the narrative.

Second, and more generally, negative depictions do not always lead to audience disassociation. Many scholars assume that the negative characterization necessarily leads to a rejection of the Twelve. However, this is not always true. Numerous studies have demonstrated that audiences often develop feelings for characters who are portrayed as violating societal norms and/or the moral standards of an artistic work.[10] Gangster, mafia, and heist narratives rou-

---

10. Iverson, *Performing Early Christian Literature*, 74–88.

tinely depict characters in such a fashion. In these contexts, it is not uncommon for audiences to develop sympathetic feelings for characters who might otherwise be viewed as unethical in the real world. It is therefore presumptuous to conclude that the audience is to reject the disciples as a consequence of the narrative depiction.

Third, and perhaps most troublesome for the previous approach, Jesus does not abandon the disciples either within the narrative or in the anticipated future beyond the narrative. At no point in Mark's story does Jesus forsake the disciples due to their continued failures, misunderstanding, resistance, or denial. Despite their shortcomings, the disciples will play a future, faithful, and courageous role in service to Jesus (13:9–13). And as a precursor to this ministry, Jesus will be reunited with the disciples after the resurrection (14:27–28). Both of these concepts—a future reunion and ministry—are particularly problematic for any view suggesting that the disciples are to be rejected. Since both promises are tied to the Markan Jesus, neither can be easily dismissed. The question thus becomes, if Mark's Jesus does not reject the disciples, why should the audience? To disassociate from the disciples puts the audience in opposition to Jesus, the central and guiding character of the narrative.

CONCLUSION

Discipleship is one of the central themes in Mark's Gospel. The complex portrait of the Twelve—a stunning and perhaps unexpected montage—vacillates between faith and following to resistance and denial, and everywhere in between. Yet Mark encourages the audience to identify with the disciples. Lest the audience fail to appreciate the demands of being a disciple, Mark crafts a narrative that exposes the challenges and struggles for all would-be followers. The portrait is not idealistic, but perhaps it offers a more relatable and authentic account for future followers of Jesus. In the end, the characterization of the Twelve beckons all disciples to consider their own fear and foolishness and to contemplate what it means to follow Jesus beyond the narrative world of Mark's Gospel.

QUESTIONS FOR REFLECTION

1. What positive characteristics are associated with the disciples?

2. What negative characteristics are associated with the disciples?

3. Why does Mark depict the disciples in such a negative fashion?

FURTHER READING

Combs, Jason Robert. "A Ghost on the Water? Understanding an Absurdity in Mark 6:49–50." *JBL* 127 (2008) 345–58.

Gibson, Jeffrey B. "The Rebuke of the Disciples in Mark 8:14–21." *JSNT* 27 (1986) 31–47.

Iverson, Kelly R. *Gentiles in the Gospel of Mark: Even the Dogs under the Table Eat the Children's Crumbs.* LNTS 339. London: T. & T. Clark, 2007.

———. *Performing Early Christian Literature: Audience Experience and Interpretation of the Gospels.* Cambridge: Cambridge University Press, 2021.

Kelber, Werner H. *The Kingdom in Mark: A New Place and a New Time.* Philadelphia: Fortress, 1974.

Malbon, Elizabeth S. *In the Company of Jesus: Characters in Mark's Gospel.* Louisville: Westminster John Knox, 2000.

———. *Narrative Space and Mythic Meaning in Mark.* New Voices in Biblical Studies. San Francisco: Harper & Row, 1986.

Tannehill, Robert C. "The Disciples in Mark: The Function of a Narrative Role." *JR* 57 (1977) 386–405.

Tyson, Joseph B. "The Blindness of the Disciples in Mark." *JBL* 80 (1961) 261–68.

Weeden, Theodore J. *Mark: Traditions in Conflict*. Philadelphia: Fortress, 1971.

Williams, Joel F. *Other Followers of Jesus: Minor Characters as Major Figures in Mark's Gospel*. JSNTSup 102. Sheffield: JSOT Press, 1994.

5

"IS A LAMP TO BE PUT UNDER A BASKET?"

Mark's Secrecy Theme

Students often assume that Mark's Gospel depicts Jesus as a transparent communicator who openly reveals his identity and mission. On first impression, the logic makes sense. Jesus calls disciples, teaches, and interacts in a public setting. While this is correct, Mark's presentation of Jesus also moves in a different direction. A close reading of the narrative reveals a pervasive theme of secrecy or, at the very least, a series of related episodes. Jesus does not allow the demons to reveal his identity; he commands those who have witnessed his miraculous deeds to remain silent; he speaks in cryptic parables; and he deliberately avoids the crowds. Indeed, the element of secrecy is a common feature in Mark's narrative (see table 5.1). The question therefore is why the narrative portrays Jesus speaking and engaging in a secretive fashion.

Table 5.1

Examples of Markan Secrecy

1:24–25: "Have you come to destroy us? I know who you are, the Holy One of God." But Jesus rebuked him, saying, "Be silent, and come out of him!"

1:34: And he cured many who were sick with various diseases, and cast out many demons; and he would not permit the demons to speak, because they knew him.

1:44: "See that you say nothing to anyone; but go, show yourself to the priest, and offer for your cleansing what Moses commanded, as a testimony to them."

3:11–12: Whenever the unclean spirits saw him, they fell down before him and shouted, "You are the Son of God!" But he sternly ordered them not to make him known.

4:11: And he said to them, "To you has been given the secret of the kingdom of God, but for those outside, everything comes in parables."

8:26: Then he sent him away to his home, saying, "Do not even go into the village."

8:30: And he sternly ordered them not to tell anyone about him.

9:9: As they were coming down the mountain, he ordered them to tell no one about what they had seen, until after the Son of Man had risen from the dead.

Mark's emphasis on secrecy has led to significant debate in the history of scholarship. Often referred to as the "messianic secret," the discussion has focused on a number of historical, theological, cultural, political, and literary issues in order to understand the use of the theme. To appreciate the breadth of the conversation the following will consider five views, each of which is shaped by a different hermeneutical perspective or way of approaching the discussion. This overview will orient students to the complexity of the issue as well as to the various ways scholars have attempted to make sense of Markan secrecy.

(1) THE MESSIANIC SECRET

In 1901, William Wrede published *The Messianic Secret*. By virtually all accounts, the book was a landmark publication. The study had sweeping implications and remains the starting point for any discussion of secrecy in Mark's Gospel, even if Wrede's conclusions are not widely accepted today.

Wrede argued that the "messianic secret" was a significant feature of the second Gospel. He suggested that the concept could be discerned in numerous Markan contexts, including Jesus's interactions with the demons (1:25, 34; 3:12), the disciples (8:30; 9:2–9), and the various supplicants encountered throughout the narrative (1:43–45; 5:37–43; 7:33–36; 8:23–26). The element of secrecy was also evident in Jesus's repeated attempts to maintain anonymity (7:24; 9:30), as well as his use of parables (4:10–13, 33). Wrede suggested that the diverse and widespread use of secrecy must be appreciated from a holistic perspective.

It was Wrede's explanation of this agenda that proved to be most controversial. Wrede argued that the use of secrecy did not originate with the historical Jesus, but instead was a theological overlay created by the early church. The reason this perspective came into existence was because, according to Wrede, Jesus never claimed to be Messiah during his earthly ministry. It was only through the resurrection that Jesus became Messiah and was acclaimed as such by his followers (Acts 2:36; Rom 1:4; Phil 2:6–11).

As time passed, the obvious question was how Jesus could be regarded as Messiah when his earthly life was lacking in "sovereign dignity and power."[1] Wrede suggested that the messianic secret was created in order to account for these two theological perspectives. It was a transitional doctrine that allowed the church to simultaneously affirm that Jesus was the Messiah even though Jesus never claimed to be the Messiah during his earthly life. The messianic secret was the christological solution to a theological dilemma: Jesus was always the Messiah, but he concealed his identity during his public ministry. This doctrinal development was a theological invention created by the early church to reconcile divergent christological perspectives in a coherent fashion.

In the history of scholarship, it is sometimes suggested that the messianic secret originated with Mark. However, Wrede argued that the use of secrecy is so interwoven in Mark's Gospel that this is unlikely. In fact, it is doubtful that Mark or any individual was the sole creator of the tradition. According to Wrede, the secret was developed by the early church, absorbed into the traditions received by the second evangelist, and eventually expressed in the narrative of Mark's Gospel. Mark was a creative theologian and accentuated the theme, but the messianic secret originated and developed long before the evangelist constructed the second Gospel. For Wrede, the evangelist was ignorant of these developments and, *"knew nothing of when Jesus was acknowledged* to be Messiah . . . [and had] absolutely no interest in this question."[2]

As one can imagine, to suggest that Jesus's messianic status was mapped onto the pre-Easter tradition drew a sharp response. Shortly after the publication of *The*

1. Wrede, *Messianic Secret*, 216–17.

2. Wrede, *Messianic Secret*, 115, emphasis original.

Messianic Secret, William Sanday concluded that "Wrede's reconstruction of the Gospel history is accepted by no one" because his "strange hypothesis" is "not only very wrong but also distinctly wrong-headed."[3] Though some softened to the approach over time, the majority of scholars did not find Wrede's hypothesis compelling—for two reasons.

First, it is not entirely clear why the resurrection would have marked a definitive point at which the early church would have declared a non-messianic Jesus to be the Messiah. In one of the defining works on the historical Jesus written in the last century, Albert Schweitzer offers an insightful response to Wrede that is worth quoting in full.

> How can the appearances of the risen Jesus have suggested to the disciples the idea that Jesus, the crucified teacher, was the Messiah? Apart from any expectations, how can this conclusion have resulted for them from the mere "fact of the resurrection"? The fact of the appearance did not by any means imply it. In certain circles, indeed, according to Mark vi. 14–16, in the very highest quarters, the resurrection of the Baptist was believed in; but that did not make John the Baptist the Messiah. The inexplicable thing is that, according to Wrede, the disciples began at once to assert confidently and unanimously that He was the Messiah and would before long appear in glory.[4]

To assume that the resurrection was the basis for acclaiming Jesus as the Messiah seems to ignore important data within the narrative. Contrary to Wrede, the resurrection only makes sense as an indicator of Jesus's messianic

3. Sanday, *Life of Christ*, 70, 75–67.

4. Schweitzer, *Quest of the Historical Jesus*, 345.

status, if the association had already been made during his earthly ministry.

The second issue with Wrede's reconstruction has to do with the coherency of the messianic secret. Wrede assumed that the concept was part of an integrated whole that expressed itself at different junctures in the narrative. Scholars have since questioned this conclusion, drawing particular attention to the unique narrative contexts. For example, Luz argues that there are two kinds of secrets in Mark's Gospel: the messianic secret and the miracle secret.[5] The messianic secret includes those scenes involving Jesus's identity, such as the commands to demons and, in the latter portion of the narrative, the disciples. The miracle secret entails those instances where—typically following a powerful deed—Jesus commands a person or crowd to remain silent. Though both categories involve an element of secrecy, the content or substance of what is hidden varies. This delineation of the messianic secret is pressed even further by Räisänen, who suggests that there are four loosely related categories of secrecy in Mark's narrative: 1) the injunctions to silence given to demons and disciples; 2) the healing narratives; 3) Jesus's parabolic speech; and 4) the disciples' lack of understanding.[6] According to Räisänen, only the first category can be described under the banner of a messianic secret.

These reflections offer a more nuanced understanding of Mark's narrative. Indeed, it is difficult to conclude that there is a messianic secret in Mark's miracle scenes. At least among the human supplicants, the deeds of Jesus rarely lead to the discernment of his identity. In Mark 6:1–3, for example, when Jesus returns to his hometown of Nazareth, the people widely acknowledge the "miracles performed

5. Luz, "Secrecy Motif," 86–87.

6. Räisänen, "'Messianic Secret' in Mark's Gospel," 132–33.

by his hands" (6:2). But despite acknowledging his power, they do not consider him to be a messianic figure, only a "carpenter, the son of Mary, and the brother of James, Joses, Judas, and Simon." It thus appears that Wrede collapsed various types of secrecy into a single secret. While Wrede was right to note the prevalence of the theme, his historical assessment was problematic and the majority of scholars no longer hold to his conclusions, even though his ground-breaking work is universally acknowledged in the history of the discussion.

(2) HONOR AND SHAME

Wrede's so-called messianic secret was thoroughly critiqued in the century after his original publication, but the concept of secrecy remained a hallmark of the discussion. In a more recent study, David Watson offers an entirely new approach.[7] Adopting a social-scientific perspective, Watson argues that the second Gospel is not concerned with secrecy per se, but with the Mediterranean values of honor and shame.

Watson lays the foundation for his study by exploring the concept of secrecy—the assumed starting point for the conversation. Watson suggests that in the Mediterranean world secrecy could be signaled through a variety of terms, including "to hide," "to creep," "not to be spoken," "to conceal," "mystery," etc.[8] What is interesting, Watson notes, is that the language of secrecy is rarely used in Mark. In fact, there are only four occasions where Mark employs this language, three of which occur at the beginning of the fourth chapter (4:11; 4:22 [2x]; 7:24).

7. Watson, *Honor among Christians.*
8. Watson, *Honor among Christians,* 20–22.

Though the linguistic survey is compelling, Watson acknowledges that the concept of secrecy may be present even if the language is not. Take, for example, the sentence "She kept this information to herself." The statement does not utilize the above-mentioned terminology, but it does convey the idea of secrecy.[9] Given this possibility, Watson considers the typical functions of secrecy in the ancient Mediterranean world. In general, Watson suggests that there are four uses of secrecy: 1) to protect from defamation, prosecution, or persecution; 2) to establish social boundaries between groups; 3) to defend an individual or group from envy and hostility; and 4) to safeguard the inexpressibility of a sacred truth. As was the case with the linguistic evidence, Watson concludes that these functional categories are largely absent from Mark's Gospel. Contrary to previous scholarship, Mark does not demonstrate an overriding concern for secrecy, either in relation to Jesus's identity, speech, or deeds. Watson argues that the concept has been misapplied to Mark's Gospel due in large part to the uncritical acceptance of Wrede's foundational work.

This, however, is not to dismiss the grouping of texts that have been identified under the banner of secrecy. Watson suggests that the primary thematic issue is not secrecy but honor and shame. In an ancient Mediterranean context where honor was valued above all else, the acquisition of public affirmation was often derived through patron-client relationships, a system of dependency between "socially superior 'patrons' and their socially inferior 'clients.'"[10] In exchange for a patron's gracious sharing of resources, the client was to reciprocate by offering honor and praise. The interchange did not necessitate the repayment of goods or

9. Watson, *Honor among Christians*, 24.

10. John H. Elliott, "Patronage and Clientage," 144, quoted in Watson, *Honor among Christians*, 43.

services, but the public elevation of the patron. For the client to fail in this unstated but obligatory duty was shameful by societal standards. Though such exchanges may seem foreign, they undergirded Mediterranean life and offer the social backdrop for Mark's Gospel.

As an illustration of these cultural norms, Watson reappraises several texts typically understood as part of the so-called messianic secret. In each of these texts, Jesus restores an individual and immediately commands the recipient to remain quiet (1:40–45; 5:21–24, 35–43; 7:31–37; 8:22–26). Watson argues that the interactions in each of these scenes must be appreciated within an ancient Mediterranean context. In Mark's Gospel, Jesus is the ultimate patron. He freely provides the gift of healing to the supplicants of the narrative. Because of this, and in accord with cultural expectations, Jesus is to receive honor and praise. However, instead of embracing this rightful honor, Jesus resists public affirmation by repeatedly commanding the supplicants of the narrative to remain silent. These episodes therefore do not hinge on the notion of secrecy but on the entrenched, societal norms of achieved honor.

A similar issue is at play when Jesus refuses to allow others to identify him with honorific titles (e.g., "the Holy One of God," "Son of God," "Son of Man"). In the ancient Mediterranean world, ascribed honor was typically derived from an individual's rank and stature. And, for those who found themselves in such a position, to embrace one's status was expected. Yet, as Watson observes, Jesus repeatedly shuns the very titles that might have advanced his social standing—once again pursuing a course that is at odds with the cultural values of the day.

This does not mean, according to Watson, that Mark is attempting to do away with cultural conventions. Rather, Mark is redefining the concepts of honor and shame. The trajectory of the narrative shapes this vision, but the teaching in Mark 8 and 10 gives explicit voice to this narrative agenda. Honor is not achieved by power, titles, elevated social status, or benefaction (10:45). Honor comes to those who are willing to serve, to be last, and to embrace the values of God's kingdom, including the cross (a symbol of shame in the ancient world [8:34–35]). Though followers of Jesus may be rejected for their allegiance to the kingdom, the promise of the gospel is that disciples will experience a future vindication. Mark's narrative inverts societal expectations and presents the audience with a new standard of honor (i.e., the way of Jesus) and shame (i.e., the way of the world).

There is much to commend in Watson's study, in particular the attempt to locate Mark's narrative within the sociocultural milieu of the first century. However, while the discussion accounts for certain features of the narrative, it does not adequately explain others. In particular, Watson focuses on instances where Jesus appears to resist achieved or ascribed honor. But there are an equal number of places where Jesus acts in a public setting and makes no attempt to disavow the kind of honor typically ascribed to patrons. For example, in Mark 3:1–6 Jesus heals a man with a withered hand without providing any command to silence. Likewise, when Jesus makes his dramatic entry into Jerusalem, riding on a donkey, and being acclaimed as the Son of David (11:10), he does not quiet the honorific chants of the raucous crowd (11:9).

To his credit, Watson addresses the issue and identifies eighteen examples where the Markan Jesus does not resist public honor (1:21–28, 29–31, 32–34; 2:1–12, 28; 3:1–6, 7–12; 4:35–41; 5:1–20, 24b–34; 6:30–44, 45–52, 53–56; 7:24–30; 8:1–9; 9:14–28, 38–41; 10:46–52). He acknowledges that there are "many passages" where Jesus "heals openly, performs mass exorcisms, shows his ability to control nature, feeds the thousands of people, and refers to himself as having authority."[11] He suggests that while there is tension, Mark is concerned with advancing a variety of themes that are equally important to the rhetorical and theological objectives of the gospel. He further argues that though this type of inconsistency may be problematic for modern interpreters, ancient audiences were far more accommodating to these narrative dynamics.

Watson's thesis is intriguing and in certain places offers helpful insight. But it does not account for a variety of texts that push in a different direction. The volume of this material is highly problematic—even though Watson acknowledges the issue and qualifies his conclusion. The fact that Mark's Jesus embraces honor as frequently as he rejects it limits the explanatory power of Watson's social-scientific hypothesis.

(3) ROMAN POLITICAL IDEOLOGY

Despite its weaknesses, Adam Winn builds on Watson's approach while simultaneously moving the conversation in a new direction.[12] Winn argues that Jesus's resistance to honor is intended to evoke Roman political ideology. In depicting Jesus in this fashion, Mark co-opts the imperial values of Rome in order to affirm that Jesus (not Caesar) is the true ruler of the world.

Winn acknowledges that "honor was one of the greatest and most prized virtues" in the ancient world.[13] And, like Watson, Winn affirms that Jesus both resists honor and

11. Watson, *Honor among Christians*, 113–14.

12. Winn, "Resisting Honor"; Winn, *Reading Mark's Christology*, 119–30.

13. Winn, "Resisting Honor," 586.

embraces honor at different points in the narrative. While there is agreement, Winn also notes Watson does not integrate these perspectives in a satisfactory manner. Instead, Winn proposes three possible paradigms to understand this multilayered portrait of Jesus.

First, Winn considers the possible influence of Cynic philosophy. The Cynics were a first-century group who were noted for their disdain of honor, material possessions, physical comfort, and social conventions. Cynics embraced poverty, ascetic practices, and acts of disgraceful public behavior. Though this description of the Cynic lifestyle is brief, it is possible to identify potential areas of convergence with Mark, including the de-emphasis on physical belongings and the rejection of honor. However, Winn rightly dismisses the parallels, arguing that other features of the narrative stand in sharp relief to conventional Cynic practices, such as the participation in social meals and Jesus's widespread public esteem.

The second possibility that Winn explores is whether Jesus's aversion to honor is an envy avoidance strategy. Honor was a desired virtue, but it was also understood as a limited good. An honor ascribed to one person necessarily implied a lack of honor for another. The inevitable distinction between individuals often gave rise to envy, a negative and potentially dangerous emotion that could result in undesirable outcomes, including physical harm. For this reason, individuals sought to obtain honor while avoiding envy. To do so, an individual could 1) use their status to benefit others; 2) act in a humble manner; 3) minimize their own honor; 4) live a life of virtue; 5) grant honor to others; 6) acknowledge honor as a gift of divine favor; and 7) engage in a self-deprecating manner. Winn argues that although some of Jesus's actions might be regarded as envy avoidance strategies (e.g., 4:36; 5:19; 7:24; 9:29; 10:18), others do not. In particular, at no point does Jesus instruct an individual to reject an honor that has been properly bestowed.

According to Winn, the third and most compelling paradigm for understanding Jesus's rejection of honor is Roman political ideology. Prior to the NT (i.e., the republican era), there was great resistance to monarchial rule in Rome, as well as the honors typically ascribed to monarchial figures. As a result, any honors that might be associated with such rule (e.g., titles, temples, divine worship) were deemed inappropriate. With the coming of Caesar Augustus (27 BCE–14 CE), however, this perspective took a dramatic turn. As the individual who possessed sole authority over Rome, Augustus began to receive unprecedented honors—the granting of which had previously been despised. In order to acknowledge the sensibilities of an age gone by, Augustus embraced a policy of *recusatio*, a strategy that allowed him to reject "the outward appearance of absolute power but not the power itself."[14] This mediating approach became the default expectation for all those who followed after Caesar Augustus.

This political context, Winn argues, provides the paradigm to understand Mark's depiction of Jesus and his selective rejection of public honors. In addition, there are three supporting factors that contribute to this conclusion. First, Winn suggests that Mark's Gospel was likely written in Rome, making it more likely that Roman readers would have naturally associated Jesus's rejection of public honors with Augustus's strategy of *recusatio*.

Second, Mark depicts Jesus as a world ruler. In fact, the opening line of the narrative describes Jesus as Messiah (1:1). This designation is reiterated on two other occasions (8:29; 14:61) and, according to Winn, has

14. Winn, "Resisting Honor," 590.

royal connotations. As ruler, Jesus is further characterized as God's Son (1:11; 9:7), a Davidic descendent (11:7–10), and the Danielic "Son of Man" (13:26; 14:62). By depicting Jesus in this fashion, Mark deliberately sets the narrative in conversation with Roman political ideology. Of the five occasions where Jesus displays an aversion to public honor, three are directly related to his being described as God's ruler (3:12; 8:28–30; 9:9).

Third, Winn argues that there is a discernible and thorough critique of Roman rule in Mark's narrative and that the characterization of Jesus intentionally parallels the vocabulary and propaganda of Rome. From the titles ascribed to Jesus to his various displays of power, Jesus is presented in the context of Roman imperial ideology. Winn suggests that Mark's aim is to challenge the claims of Rome by intentionally using the language of Rome. The purpose of this rhetorical strategy is to affirm that Jesus, not Caesar, is the one true ruler of the world. Jesus's resistance to honor exemplifies what is virtuous about Rome's imperial values, even as the narrative seeks to undermine the gospel of Rome while advancing the kingdom of God.

Winn suggests that this approach to Markan secrecy rectifies the deficiencies in Watson's more general honor/shame hypothesis. In particular, the problem of balancing secrecy and publicity is alleviated by situating the discussion in the context of Roman political ideology. Roman rulers were expected to embrace *recusatio*, but individuals were not expected to distance themselves from all public honors. Only excessive honors were to be rejected. Against this backdrop, Winn suggests that Mark's depiction of Jesus falls squarely in line with the Roman practice of *recusatio*.

Winn's approach to Markan secrecy adds a new perspective and seemingly avoids some of the pitfalls associated with Watson's social-scientific interpretation. However, it is questionable whether the solution accounts for the totality of Mark's narrative. Winn maintains that the "[r]esistance to public honor was a means by which the emperor drew a line between appropriate and excessive honor."[15] This distinction is important because it seemingly accounts for the acceptance and rejection of honor in Mark's narrative. But if this is the case, it is not apparent how or where Jesus maintains this line of demarcation. For example, in Mark 7:31–37 Jesus heals a man with a speech impediment. After the man is restored, Jesus instructs those present to tell no one about the event. In a similar narrative, Jesus heals an anonymous woman suffering from a hemorrhage (5:24–34). A large crowd is present, but Jesus does not silence the woman or the crowd after the display of power. How is the interpreter to account for these differences? Why is one group commanded to be silent and the other is not? What specifically accounts for Jesus's response in each of these episodes?

Or to state it differently, how does Mark 5:24–34 represent an "appropriate" honor, while 7:31–37 is an "excessive" honor? Even more generally, how is the interpreter to discern between "appropriate" and "excessive" honors throughout the narrative? Winn's thesis is predicated on the qualification, but the discussion offers little assistance in addressing this foundational question. Without additional clarification, one is left with the impression that the distinction is somewhat arbitrary. In the end, more work needs to be done to assess whether Mark discriminates between "appropriate" and "excessive" honors in the narrative.

15. Winn, *Reading Mark's Christology*, 130.

(4) A NARRATIVE TENSION

The previous interpretations have considered certain historical/theological, cultural, or political features behind the text in order to understand the use of secrecy in Mark. Malbon refocuses the discussion on the text of Mark's Gospel to consider the theme from a distinctly literary perspective.[16] Malbon suggests that there is a creative tension in the narrative that helps account for the narrative use of secrecy.

Malbon lays the groundwork for her study by exploring two issues in the interpretation of narrative. First, Malbon notes that characters are revealed through their words and deeds, as well as by the words and deeds of others (including other characters and the narrator). This preliminary and rather uncontentious observation aside, Malbon moves to a second and more disputed issue. Malbon suggests that there is a crucial distinction between the implied author and the narrator. In literary studies, the implied author is the one assumed to be responsible for the narrative, including the shape of the text, the development of characters, and the points of view expressed in the story.[17] The narrator, on the other hand, is the one who tells the story from within a literary work. Though the narrator may function "above" the characters in the story, the narrator is a character-like figure who expresses a particular point of view and is controlled by the implied author. Though these distinctions are subtle, Malbon argues that scholars have

16. Malbon, "History, Theology, Story." See also Malbon, *Mark's Jesus*.

17. The author is the flesh and blood individual(s) who is responsible for the composition of a text. Because scholars have little access to these historical persons (see ch. 1), narrative critics often refer to the implied author. The implied author is a literary construct based solely on information that can be deduced about the author from the text.

too frequently assumed that "Jesus, the narrator, and the implied author share the same point of view in Mark."[18]

In light of these methodological observations, Malbon next analyzes the characters in the narrative who identify Jesus using various titles and descriptors. The demons recognize Jesus as "the Holy One of God" (1:24), the "Son of God" (3:11), and the "Son of the Most High God" (5:7). John the Baptist identifies Jesus as "the one more powerful than I" (1:7). Peter confesses Jesus to be the "Messiah" (8:29), and the heavenly voice twice uses the language of sonship (1:11; 9:7). Taken together, these statements describe Jesus using theologically elevated language, communicating what Malbon suggests is a "projected" Christology—a view of Jesus based on the perspective of others.

Malbon argues that there is a "significant gap" between Mark's projected Christology and what Jesus says about himself (enacted Christology).[19] Unlike other characters in the narrative, Jesus does not refer to himself using the same theological language. When the narrative is examined in detail, "the words of the Markan Jesus fail to echo the words" of the demons, the disciples, the crowds, and others.[20] Moreover, Jesus often prohibits other characters from speaking about his identity and therefore employing Mark's projected Christology. Although this distinction has been underappreciated in Markan studies, Malbon suggests that it is significant for understanding the narrative.

Building on these insights, Malbon argues that Mark's Gospel does not reveal a "messianic secret" or even a secrecy theme. Instead, the narrative portrays a Jesus who is inherently shy and reserved. Consider two examples. In Mark 1:39–45 Jesus travels through Galilee and encounters

18. Malbon, "History, Theology, Story," 44.

19. Malbon, "History, Theology, Story," 45.

20. Malbon, "History, Theology, Story," 45.

a leper in need of healing. After cleansing the man, Jesus instructs him to tell no one but to go offer sacrifices to God. A similar type of scene occurs in Mark 5:1–20 when Jesus heals a demon-possessed man. After the exorcism, Jesus commands the man to return home and tell "how much the Lord has done" (5:19). Although both of these passages have been used to illustrate Markan secrecy, Malbon argues that they more accurately reflect Jesus's tendency to divert attention away from himself. This "shyness," depicted at numerous places in the narrative, exemplifies Mark's "deflected" Christology. Jesus consistently attempts to move the spotlight of attention away from himself and towards the character of God.

When all of the pieces to Mark's puzzle are considered, the text's deflected Christology and projected Christology do not fully align. What the characters in the story convey about Jesus is not conveyed by the Markan Jesus. Malbon suggests that even the narrator's point of view is to be distinguished from the character of Jesus. As evidence, Malbon points to the opening verse of the Gospel in which the narrator identifies Jesus as the Son of God (1:1). This christological affirmation is never proclaimed by Jesus and only reluctantly accepted at the Jewish trial (14:61–62). While the narrator focuses almost exclusively on the character of Jesus, the character of Jesus consistently focuses on the character of God.

There is thus a tension between the character of Jesus and the other characters/narrator in Mark's story. This is not to suggest that the vantage points are completely at odds or incompatible. In some instances, a perspective that is expressed by Jesus is later articulated by the narrator. After Jesus commands an unclean spirit to be silent in Capernaum (1:25), the narrator goes on to provide a summary account that reaffirms these actions (1:34). In other instances, a view expressed by the narrator is later articulated by Jesus. In the prologue to Mark's Gospel, the narrator joins together Scripture, Elijah, and John the Baptist (1:2–8). The same conglomeration of ideas is repeated by Jesus in the transfiguration scene (9:11–13). Malbon suggests that the few occasions where these overlaps do occur are the exception rather than the rule. The tension between the Markan Jesus and the characters/narrator is a persistent feature across the whole of the narrative and it is the audience who must hold together Mark's various christological perspectives.

There is much to appreciate in Malbon's work. Her discussion offers a new and fascinating interpretation of Mark's Gospel. But there are two lingering issues that arise from the study. First, although there are instances where Malbon's reading is convincing, it does not explain the entire Gospel, particularly those scenes where Jesus is not reserved or shy. Not infrequently, the Markan Jesus engages in discussion or performs a deed without redirecting the focus of attention. In one noteworthy example (2:1–12), a paralyzed man is lowered through a roof and into a house in order to be healed. When Jesus witnesses the act of faith, he declares the man forgiven, causing the religious leaders to ponder, "Who can forgive sins but God alone?" (2:7). Although Jesus perceives the religious leaders' inner thoughts, he makes no attempt to clarify that God alone is the forgiver of sin. Instead, Jesus affirms that *he* has the authority to forgive sins as the Son of Man (2:10). Though Malbon is right to draw attention to Mark's deflected Christology, this does not appear to be a universal phenomenon. The inconsistencies in the narrative problematize Malbon's assessment of the secrecy or shyness theme.

The second issue stems from Malbon's contention that the narrator communicates a point of view that is to be differentiated from the implied author. To be sure, modern literary critics do make this distinction and contemporary narratives are known to exploit these differences. However, it is questionable whether ancient narratives like the Gospel of Mark made use of this potential. Unfortunately, Malbon does not provide any examples to justify the assertion. Moreover, in an ancient context where the Gospel was performed, it is difficult to appreciate how an audience might distinguish between the implied author and the narrator. The more natural assumption would be that the performer/narrator is an extension of and voice for the implied author. While Malbon's narrative approach is intriguing, it may resonate with modern literary techniques more so than with ancient media practices.

(5) AN AUDIENCE-ELEVATING DEVICE

The final interpretation understands Mark's secrecy theme to be an audience-elevating device.[21] The use of the theme is for the benefit of the audience and for the advancement of Mark's narrative aims. When appreciated in performance, the concept has a functional purpose that serves a broader theological agenda.

To a certain extent, this view grows out of a dissatisfaction with traditional approaches to the question of Markan secrecy. Despite variation, scholars have sought to address the issue by adopting a singular concept that probes either behind the text (historical, cultural, or political) or within the text (narratival). While these perspectives are helpful, each seeks to interpret the narrative by proposing a universal concept to account for the peculiarities of Mark's Gospel. As the previous analysis has shown, the theme is sufficiently complex to defy such an explanation. Just as the

21. Iverson, "Wherever the Gospel Is Preached."

"messianic" secret was unable to account for the diversity of the narrative, neither have contemporary approaches been able to address the breadth of Mark's Gospel. When viewed holistically, the narrative resists a one-size-fits-all explanation, at least as the discussion has traditionally been framed.

Rather than focusing on what is behind or within the text, it may be helpful to consider what is in front of the text. It is possible that the use of secrecy is driven by broader theological and performative interests.[22] This suggestion is based, in part, on an understanding of the default communicative medium. For most in the first century, traditions like Mark's Gospel were communicated in an oral setting. The vast majority of individuals did not possess written manuscripts nor were they able to read extended narratives like Mark's Gospel. This communication reality necessitated a Gospel "performance" (i.e., a public reading and/or dramatic presentation) before a live audience in a shared, relational space. The appreciation of this communicative medium reframes how the interpreter might approach the question of Markan secrecy. Instead of asking how secrecy functions within the narrative, perhaps it would be profitable to explore how secrecy functions within the dynamics of a performance event.

To appreciate this perspective, it is important to distinguish between the use of the theme in the narrative and the audience's experience of the secrecy in performance. For both the characters and the audience, secrecy is repeatedly brought to the fore of the narrative. Jesus does not allow the

22. For the reasons mentioned above, I am not convinced that Mark's secrecy theme is a veiled reference to honor and shame, either generally or in terms of a political agenda. Regardless of one's assessment, these approaches do not preclude the notion of secrecy. It is possible that the Markan Jesus uses secrecy to resist honorific titles and acclamations.

demons to speak; he avoids crowds; and he is not explicit about his identity. All of these actions represent behaviors that surround the ministry of Jesus. For the characters in the narrative, the use of the theme often prohibits them from understanding who Jesus is or what his teaching is ultimately about.

Unlike the characters in the narrative, there are no secrets for the audience of Mark's Gospel. The audience is a silent listener to every conversation and possesses a semi-omniscient (i.e., almost all-knowing) perspective via the narrator. From the opening of the Gospel, the audience is informed that Jesus is the Christ and Son of God (1:1). While the characters in the narrative grapple with Jesus's identity, the audience is afforded a unique perspective through performance. This distinct vantage point provides the audience with privileged information that is not available to each of the characters in the narrative. Although secrecy permeates elements of the narrative world, it does not conceal the mysteries of the Gospel from the audience.

This discrepancy is a common rhetorical technique in both ancient and modern media. Sometimes referred to as an audience-elevating strategy, this type of technique adds suspense, creates tension, and stimulates audience interest. Since the audience shares the narrator's perspective, the audience is ever, if always, a step ahead of the characters. This differentiation between the audience and characters produces a level of drama that creates intrigue and piques audience interest. That Mark utilizes techniques of this kind is not in doubt and is widely affirmed by Markan scholars.

But it may be that there is more at stake in a theologically oriented text like Mark's narrative, particularly when the Gospel is appreciated as a performance event. Mark is concerned in telling a good story, but it is not simply another story that Mark is telling. The narrative has been crafted to compel the audience to embrace a particular vision of the world—a theological perspective that Mark deeply affirms and wants to convey. The widespread use of secrecy contributes to this purpose and, though it adds a sense of drama to the unfolding events, it is likely motivated by a broader theological concern.

To understand how Mark accomplishes this theological agenda requires a slight digression. In performance, the relationship between a performer and audience is crucial and often shapes the outcome of a communicative event. Of the many influences on this relationship, one that is particularly relevant to the present discussion is the "disclosure/liking" effect.[23] This fairly intuitive principle suggests that there is a positive relationship between disclosure and liking. As long as such acts of disclosure are culturally appropriate, personal revelation generally has a positive effect on relational development. The rationale for this is that "when people perceive that they have been personally selected for intimate discourse, they feel trusted and liked and are more apt to evaluate the discloser favorably."[24] Disclosure ultimately communicates a level of confidence in the one to whom the information is revealed. This in turn encourages positive feelings, which further stimulates the disclosure/liking process and nourishes relationships.

Returning to Mark, the disclosure/liking effect is important because it undergirds the performance event, which consequently affects the reception of the Gospel. To the attuned audience member, it is readily apparent that many of the characters do not possess the same level of insight, if any at all. Yet for the audience, the struggle experienced by the characters is overcome through performance. Because of the repeated and deliberate acts of performative disclosure, the

23. Iverson, "Wherever the Gospel Is Preached," 203–4.

24. Collins and Miller, "Self-Disclosure and Liking," 459.

audience is consistently offered access to the mysteries that confound the characters in the story. This built-in rhetorical device facilitates the disclosure/liking effect and fosters the relational dynamics between performer and audience.

The trust accrued by the performer is not without purpose and is linked to the theological aims of the narrative (13:10; 14:9). By revealing the secrets of the kingdom, the performer is able to encourage a favorable relationship with the audience. This is not to advance the reputation of the performer, but to leverage the performer's status for the Gospel itself. The theme of secrecy contributes to Mark's theological aim by influencing the perception of the performer. Since the reception of the message is closely aligned with the reception of the messenger, the relationship between performer and audience plays a crucial role in Mark's agenda. The use of secrecy facilitates the disclosure/ liking relationship, which in turn influences the reception of Mark's Gospel. Ironically, the paradoxical use of secrecy functions in service to Mark's theological vision.

The advantage of this approach to understanding Mark's Gospel is twofold. First, it is able to lay aside a perennial problem in Markan studies, while still moving the conversation forward. To date, no interpretation has been able to explain Jesus's secretive and public actions in the narrative. Second, this approach takes the performative context seriously, appreciating that Mark's theological concerns are closely intertwined with the dynamics of performance. Whatever the reason(s) for Mark's depiction in the narrative, secrecy has a powerful effect on performance. The dynamics of the oral event allow the performer to advance the Gospel by tapping into age-old, relational strategies. The secrecy theme is an audience-elevating device, deployed in the hope that all who experience the Gospel will likewise embrace Mark's vision of the world.

<table>
<tr><td colspan="3" align="center">Table 5.2
Approaches to Mark's Secrecy Theme</td></tr>
<tr><td>Scholar</td><td>Approach</td><td>Overview</td></tr>
<tr><td>William Wrede</td><td>Historical</td><td>The messianic secret was a theological concept developed by the early church to explain why Jesus never claimed to be Messiah during his ministry.</td></tr>
<tr><td>David Watson</td><td>Social-Scientific</td><td>Jesus does not act in secret, but deflects public/social honor away from himself.</td></tr>
<tr><td>Adam Winn</td><td>Political</td><td>Jesus resists excessive honors according to the Roman political practice of recusatio.</td></tr>
<tr><td>Elizabeth Struthers Malbon</td><td>Literary</td><td>Secrecy is a narrative tension that accentuates the difference between what the characters say about Jesus and what a reserved Jesus says about himself.</td></tr>
<tr><td>Kelly Iverson</td><td>Performance</td><td>The use of secrecy is an audience-elevating device used in performance to entice the audience to embrace Mark's theological worldview.</td></tr>
</table>

CONCLUSION

On various occasions, the Markan Jesus silences demons, communicates in parables, and instructs individuals to refrain from speaking. The term "messianic secret" may be a misnomer, but these texts share a degree of similarity that raises important questions about their relatedness and rationale.

Over the years, scholars have proposed a number of solutions to explain the dilemma (table 5.2). Many of these interpretations have relied on different hermeneutical perspectives, exploring various historical, cultural, literary, and performance issues. The inherent challenge has and continues to be the appreciation of Mark's entire Gospel. Despite a century of scholarly discussion, narrating a comprehensive solution has proven to be a frustrating endeavor. It appears that the question originally posed by Wrede is still with us and will likely remain a focal point of discussion for years to come.

QUESTIONS FOR REFLECTION

1. Identify two ways in which the secrecy theme has been interpreted in Mark's Gospel.

2. Why is it challenging to determine how secrecy functions in the story?

3. How does secrecy potentially affect the way Mark's narrative is received in performance?

FURTHER READING

Iverson, Kelly R. "'Wherever the Gospel Is Preached': The Paradox of Secrecy in the Gospel of Mark." In *Mark as Story: Retrospect and Prospect*, edited by Kelly R. Iverson and Christopher W. Skinner, 181–210. Resources for Biblical Studies 65. Atlanta: SBL, 2011.

Luz, Ulrich. "The Secrecy Motif and the Marcan Christology." In *The Messianic Secret*, edited by Christopher Tuckett, 75–96. IRT 1. Philadelphia: Fortress, 1983.

Malbon, Elizabeth Struthers. "History, Theology, Story: Re-Contextualizing Mark's 'Messianic Secret.'" In *Character Studies and the Gospel of Mark*, edited by Christopher W. Skinner and Matthew Ryan Hauge, 35–56. LNTS 483. London: Bloomsbury, 2014.

———. *Mark's Jesus: Characterization as Narrative Christology*. Waco, TX: Baylor University Press, 2009.

Räisänen, Heikki. "The 'Messianic Secret' in Mark's Gospel." In *The Messianic Secret*, edited by Christopher Tuckett, 132–40. IRT 1. Philadelphia: Fortress, 1983.

Schweitzer, Albert. *The Quest of the Historical Jesus*. Translated by W. Montgomery et al. Minneapolis: Fortress, 2001.

Watson, David F. *Honor among Christians: The Cultural Key to the Messianic Secret*. Minneapolis: Fortress, 2010.

Winn, Adam. *Reading Mark's Christology under Caesar: Jesus the Messiah and the Roman Imperial Ideology*. Downers Grove, IL: InterVarsity, 2018.

————. "Resisting Honor: The Markan Secrecy Motif and Roman Political Ideology." *JBL* 133 (2014) 583–601.

Wrede, William. *The Messianic Secret*. Translated by J. C. G. Greig. Library of Theological Translations. Cambridge: Clarke, 1971.

6

"HOW LONG MUST I BE WITH YOU?"

Mark's Ending

Beginnings and endings are important in narrative works. They set the stage, offer an opening or concluding thought, and orient the interpreter to the narrative as a whole. Though there is no formula to begin or end a literary text, it is often the case that their interpretive significance is disproportionate to their narrative length.

The second Gospel begins in a straightforward manner, but the conclusion to Mark's story is decidedly more complex. There are a number of issues that make the discussion of Mark's ending one of the most challenging and contested issues in the entire NT. First, it is not even clear *where* Mark ends. Ancient manuscripts reveal a number of possible conclusions to Mark's Gospel. Second, assessing these variants raises a host of textual, literary, grammatical, and historical questions that must be addressed. Third, after evaluating the textual evidence, the interpreter must then determine how the ending functions in the larger scope of Mark's story. Given the breadth of these issues, it is not surprising that Mark's ending has sometimes been described as "the greatest of all literary mysteries."[1]

The objective of this chapter is to overview several key elements of the debate. More specifically, the following discussion will 1) outline the available textual evidence; 2) evaluate the possible endings to Mark's Gospel; and 3) consider how the preferred ending might be interpreted in light of the wider narrative. Because the discussion is inherently broad and ties together various strands of the narrative, the analysis will integrate important conversations from the previous chapters.

THE TEXTUAL EVIDENCE

The starting point for any discussion of Mark's ending is the text itself. Where exactly does the Gospel conclude? In different manuscripts, Mark's story of Jesus concludes at different places. In fact, there are five unique endings to Mark's Gospel in the manuscript tradition.[2]

---

1. Nineham, *St. Mark*, 439.

2. After the Gospel stories were written down, they soon began to circulate. The "publication" of these texts came through scribal transmission (a laborious process until the invention of the printing press [1440]). Since this was not a mechanized process, it was not uncommon for scribes to alter texts. Some of these changes were made for theological reasons (i.e., intentionally), while others arose as an accidental by-product of the transmission process (i.e., unintentionally). In either case, variants were introduced into the tradition and can be observed by comparing existing manuscripts.

1. Abrupt Ending: Two of the oldest and most reliable manuscripts (א B) conclude with the so-called "abrupt ending" (16:8). After the women visit the tomb on the first day of the week, an angelic messenger informs the women that they are to tell the disciples and Peter that Jesus will meet them in Galilee. The women leave the tomb and "said nothing to anyone for they were afraid" (16:8). The end.

2. Longer Ending: The majority of ancient manuscripts (e.g., A C D K W Γ Δ Θ *f*13 28 33 𝔐) include what is often referred to as the "longer ending" (16:9–20). This ending is enshrined in most English translations of the Bible and is often placed in brackets to indicate the uncertainty of the reading. This ending follows immediately after 16:8 and extends the narrative beyond the women's fear and flight.

> Now after he rose early on the first day of the week, he appeared first to Mary Magdalene, from whom he had cast out seven demons. She went out and told those who had been with him, while they were mourning and weeping. But when they heard that he was alive and had been seen by her, they would not believe it. After this he appeared in another form to two of them, as they were walking into the country. And they went back and told the rest, but they did not believe them. Later he appeared to the eleven themselves as they were sitting at the table; and he upbraided them for their lack of faith and stubbornness, because they had not believed those who saw him after he had risen. And he said to them, "Go into all the world and proclaim the good news to the whole creation. The one who believes and is baptized will be saved; but the one who does not believe will be

condemned. And these signs will accompany those who believe: by using my name they will cast out demons; they will speak in new tongues; they will pick up snakes in their hands, and if they drink any deadly thing, it will not hurt them; they will lay their hands on the sick, and they will recover." So then the Lord Jesus, after he had spoken to them, was taken up into heaven and sat down at the right hand of God. And they went out and proclaimed the good news everywhere, while the Lord worked with them and confirmed the message by the signs that accompanied it. (16:9–20)

3. Shorter Ending: Another tradition (k) records what is known as the "shorter ending." This comparatively brief conclusion is not unlike the longer ending. The shorter ending picks up where the abrupt ending leaves off, rounding off the narrative to provide resolution to the expected reunion between Jesus and the disciples.

> And all that had been commanded them they told briefly to those around Peter. And afterward Jesus himself sent out through them, from east to west, the sacred and imperishable proclamation of eternal salvation.

4. Shorter + Longer Ending: A few manuscripts combine the shorter and longer endings (L Ψ). In these versions, the abrupt ending (16:8) is followed first by the shorter ending and then by the longer ending.

5. Freer Logion + Longer Ending: The fifth and final ending to Mark's Gospel includes the longer ending along with a tradition referred to as the Freer Logion. Named after the individual who purchased the manuscript, the Freer Logion occurs in a single text (W) and

includes an additional unit that is inserted between vv. 14 and 15 of the longer ending. The text of the Freer Logion is as follows:

> And they excused themselves, saying, "This age of lawlessness and unbelief is under Satan, who does not allow the truth and power of God to prevail over the unclean things of the spirits [*or*, does not allow what lies under the unclean spirits to understand the truth and power of God]. Therefore reveal your righteousness now"—thus they spoke to Christ. And Christ replied to them, "The term of years for Satan's power has been fulfilled, but other terrible things draw near. And for those who have sinned I was delivered over to death, that they may return to the truth and sin no more; that they may inherit the spiritual and incorruptible glory of righteousness which is in heaven."[3]

Table 6.1

Endings to Mark's Gospel

Textual Variant	Evidence	Characteristics
1. Abrupt Ending	Oldest MSS	Ends at 16:8
2. Longer Ending	Majority of MSS	Includes 16:9–20
3. Shorter Ending	One MS	Extends slightly beyond 16:8
4. Shorter + Longer Ending	Few MSS	Combines readings 2 and 3
5. Freer Logion + Longer Ending	One MS	Insertion after v. 14 of reading 2

For many students who are new to the study of the Gospels (or the Bible, in general), this evidence is rather

3. Metzger, *Textual Commentary*, 104.

startling. How can there be five endings to Mark's Gospel? And, more importantly, what is the original version? Unfortunately, we do not possess the original text of Mark's Gospel (or of any biblical text). All we have are the later manuscripts that contain the five traditions noted above—all of which were likely regarded as Scripture by certain communities. While affirming these variants, it is also true that the Gospel was presumably composed with a single conclusion. Determining where and how the narrative originally ended has been the subject of considerable debate.

EVALUATING THE EVIDENCE

In all practicality, sorting through the manuscript evidence is not quite as complicated as it might seem. Readings 3 and 4 both involve the shorter ending and may be grouped together. Neither reading is widely attested, and the shorter ending makes use of language that is not congruent with Mark's style. Consequently, readings 3 and 4 have never been given serious consideration in the history of the discussion. Reading 5 is also minimally attested and likewise employs language that is unlike the rest of the Gospel. Thus, of the five variants, readings 3, 4, and 5 were likely added at some point after the initial composition of Mark and are not original.

The Abrupt and Longer Ending

This leaves two main possibilities: 1) the abrupt ending, which concludes on a note of fear and failure (16:8); or 2) the longer ending, which narrates the response of Mary Magdalene, as well as the restoration and commission of the disciples (16:9–20). In terms of the manuscript evidence, the longer ending is supported by the overwhelming majority of texts and is well represented across a wide geographical region dating from the fifth century onwards. By contrast, the abrupt ending is found in only two major manuscripts. But these two manuscripts represent some of the earliest (fourth century) and most reliable NT textual traditions. In this respect, the manuscript evidence is somewhat divided. The majority of available manuscripts support the longer ending, but the oldest manuscripts support the abrupt ending. This problematizes the issue and pushes the conversation beyond the manuscripts themselves.

In addition to the external evidence (i.e., the manuscripts), scholars also consider the internal evidence—that is, the actual wording, style, and characteristics of the different readings. Again, the evidence is conflicting. The longer ending is problematic as it begins with an awkward transition between 16:8 and 16:9–20. Although three women—Mary Magdalene, Mary the mother of James, and Salome—are introduced at the tomb in 16:1, only Mary Magdalene appears in v. 9. Besides the curious disappearance of the two women, Mary Magdalene is reintroduced as if she were a new character, when in fact she is present throughout vv. 1–8. In addition, the text describes Mary Magdalene as the one from whom Jesus had cast out seven demons (16:9). This is unusual since only Luke mentions this particular detail (8:2). Finally, the longer ending contains a number of terms and expressions that are non-Markan and/or appear in the other Synoptic Gospels.[4]

The abrupt ending is not without difficulty as well. Why does a story of good news (1:1) conclude with what appears to be bad news? How do the women's fear and flight (16:8) offer a satisfying conclusion to Mark's story of Jesus? Why does the text break off mid-sentence with an awkward

---

4. Metzger, *Textual Commentary*, 104.

grammatical construction? Why is there no reunion with the disciples, particularly since the meeting is anticipated by Jesus (14:28) and mentioned in the second to last verse of the Gospel (16:7)? And why is there no resurrection appearance, given the repeated and explicit references to Jesus rising again (8:31; 9:31; 10:32–34)? These troublesome questions suggest that neither reading presents the interpreter with an obvious choice.

In view of this inconclusive evidence, it comes as no surprise that both readings have been affirmed at different points in history. For over eighteen hundred years, the longer ending was generally accepted as the original conclusion to Mark's Gospel. During the nineteenth century, however, scholars began to reconsider the evidence thanks to the discovery of new manuscripts. Today, the majority of scholars no longer regard vv. 9–20 to be the original conclusion. This is not because of the unusual reference to snake handling and drinking deadly poison in the longer ending (16:18). Rather it is the challenge of explaining the longer ending *in light of the abrupt ending.*[5]

If the longer ending is original, how did the abrupt ending come about? To affirm that the longer ending is the authentic conclusion, one has to assume that the last twelve verses of Mark (16:9–20) were somehow lost or removed at an extremely early date.[6] But how would this have happened? Why would a scribe intentionally omit the conclusion to Mark's Gospel? For what purpose would this serve?

5. When attempting to evaluate variants (a practice known as textual criticism), it is often assumed that the earlier or more original reading is best able to account for the development of a tradition. The logic behind this principle is that variants typically arose for discernible reasons, whether intentionally or unintentionally. To adjudicate between variants, scholars typically preference the reading that best explains the rise of the others.

6. See Farmer, *Last Twelve Verses.*

Even more problematic, this runs against the evidence. The earliest manuscripts do not include the longer ending. Why then should the interpreter assume that vv. 9–20 were omitted from the earliest manuscripts when they were not included in them originally?

For the vast majority of scholars, the longer ending is a secondary addition produced in response to the abrupt ending. Since many scribes found the abrupt ending to be inadequate, vv. 9–20 were created to complete Mark's Gospel based on a knowledge of other traditions (e.g., 1 Cor 15) and/or the other Gospels (Matt 28; Luke 24). The longer ending was designed to correct a perceived deficiency and to offer a more satisfactory conclusion to Mark's Gospel. This variant soon made its way into the manuscript tradition and quickly became the default version of Mark's ending.

This hypothesis not only accounts for the awkward transition between vv. 8 and 9, and the non-Markan language in vv. 9–20, it also explains the longer ending's dependence on other Gospel traditions. When all the data is considered, it appears that the longer ending arose in the decades after Mark was originally composed. Though it is important to acknowledge the sacredness of vv. 9–20, the evidence suggests that the longer ending was "almost certainly not penned by Mark."[7]

The Abrupt Ending: Three Possibilities

Thus far it has been shown that of the five endings to Mark's Gospel, three lack significant manuscript support (readings 3, 4, and 5) and one—though well attested—appears to be a later scribal addition (reading 2). One might assume that we have reached the end of the discussion. But affirming the

7. Marcus, *Mark 8–16*, 1088.

abrupt ending does not solve the riddle of Mark's ending. There are three further possibilities to consider: 1) Mark's narrative originally extended beyond 16:8 and included a resurrection account and/or reunion scene that has since been lost; 2) the author was prevented from completing the manuscript due to persecution, death, etc.; or 3) the narrative was intentionally composed to end in an abrupt fashion.

First, it is possible that the conclusion to Mark's Gospel was lost. Either the pages to the codex (i.e., book) fell out or the end of the scroll broke off. Though possible, this may not offer the most reasonable explanation. In order to adopt this position, one must also assume that the author passed away shortly after the writing of the text and before the manuscript had circulated to a widespread audience. Otherwise, the author and/or those familiar with the tradition could have restored the lost ending. And, if the text had already been copied, there is a greater likelihood that the original conclusion would have been preserved in the manuscript tradition. To be plausible, the final section of Mark's Gospel must have been lost during an extremely narrow window of time, shortly after the text was composed and before it began to circulate or become well known in the early church.

Second, some have argued that the abrupt ending was not the intended conclusion to Mark's Gospel. The final verse (v. 8) represents the end of the narrative only because the author was precluded from finishing the text due to an unknown life event, for example, death, persecution, or imprisonment. Of course, there are any number of circumstances that may have hindered the completion of the narrative. Such a theory is certainly possible. But the question is whether this represents the most reasonable solution. Unfortunately, there is no evidence to support this view. There are no traditions about Mark—in any known text—that would suggest that the second Gospel was left incomplete. Therefore, why should the interpreter default to speculation when another more likely solution exists?

Third, given the limitations of the previous approaches, it turns out that the simplest solution is the best solution (Occam's razor). The majority of scholars now affirm that the abrupt ending is the intended conclusion to Mark's narrative. The Gospel concludes at the place where the oldest and most reliable manuscripts indicate. Though abrupt, the ending is not an accident of history or unfortunate circumstance. The strange and unusual conclusion reflects a deliberate narrative choice by the author. Why Mark may have crafted the narrative this way will be considered in the closing section of the chapter. For now, it is important to consider two objections to this "new consensus."[8]

Objections to the Abrupt Ending

It has often been asserted that the abrupt ending is unusual, indeed highly unusual, when compared to other ancient narratives. Most narratives, it is argued, offer some form of resolution to the drama they tell. The end of a story draws the various thematic strands into a coherent and satisfying conclusion. But in Mark's Gospel there is no soft landing place at the end of the narrative. There is no resurrection appearance, no indication of what the women do after leaving the tomb, and no reunion with the disciples in Galilee. These lingering plot lines create something of an anomaly that is without significant precedent in the ancient world.

While a frequent objection, several studies have demonstrated that open and abrupt endings are not without

8. Croy, *Mutilation of Mark's Gospel*, 27.

parallel in Hebrew, Greek, and Roman literature.[9] As a case in point, there are several examples within the biblical traditions themselves. Perhaps the most famous example comes from the book of Jonah, a text that narrates the story of a prophet who is commissioned by God to go to the city of Nineveh to preach a message of repentance. At first, Jonah disobeys and boards a ship headed to the city of Tarshish. When God sends a fierce storm, Jonah is thrown overboard and swallowed by a large sea creature before eventually being spit up on dry ground. He then travels to Nineveh and preaches a message of repentance. But when the people of the city respond in genuine remorse, Jonah becomes angry.

In the closing scene of the book, Jonah withdraws from the city and begs for God to take his life. As Jonah pouts over his circumstances, the final verse of the book concludes with God's question: "And should I not be concerned about Nineveh, that great city, in which there are more than a hundred and twenty thousand persons who do not know their right hand from their left, and also many animals?" (4:11). This, it must be admitted, is a strange way to end a narrative. The reader is not told what happened to the city of Nineveh or to the prophet Jonah. The book simply ends with an unanswered question. Though there are differences between Jonah and Mark, both conclude on a note of dramatic inconclusion.

Similar endings are observable in the NT. For example, in the latter portion of Acts the narrative focuses on the ministry of Paul. The author describes Paul's various travels that eventually lead to his arrest in Acts 21. From there the narrative plots a course to Rome, precipitated by Paul's appeal to stand trial before Caesar (Acts 25:11). Paul's movements are narrated as he makes the journey,

9. Magness, *Sense and Absence*; Hooker, *Endings*; Troftgruben, *Conclusion Unhindered*.

including a disastrous shipwreck during a violent storm (Acts 27:14–44). After Paul finally arrives in Rome, the narrative concludes with these thoughts: "He [Paul] lived there two whole years at his own expense and welcomed all who came to him, proclaiming the kingdom of God and teaching about the Lord Jesus Christ with all boldness and without hindrance" (Acts 28:30–31). While there is a summative quality to these verses, they hardly bring resolution to the final chapters of Acts. What happened to Paul?! What came about from his appeal to Caesar? Was he exonerated, condemned, or something else? As before, there is a lack of finality that is reminiscent of Mark.

It would therefore appear that Mark's conclusion is not without literary parallel, but it should also be observed that there are similar examples *within* the second Gospel. For instance, as Jesus and the disciples make their way across the Sea of Galilee in 4:35–41, a fierce storm threatens to sink the boat. After Jesus calms the storm and rebukes the disciples for their lack of faith, the scene concludes with the disciples' unanswered question: "Who then is this that even the wind and the sea obey him?" (4:41). Shortly thereafter, the disciples again find themselves in the midst of a storm on the sea (6:45–51). This time, however, Jesus remains behind to pray. As the disciples struggle to make headway in the boat, Jesus comes to the disciples walking on the water. The episode concludes, noting only that the disciples had not gained any insight from the incident of the loaves (6:52). Though in some respects these scenes might be distinguished from Mark's ending, they nonetheless illustrate a kind of openness found at various junctures throughout the Gospel.

This brief selection, though not exhaustive, suggests that Mark's ending is not without precedent. Although many, if not most, ancient narratives produced closure, it is not the case that all ancient narratives followed this pattern. To suggest that the abrupt ending cannot be the final, intended verse of the Gospel ignores an array of texts that share a similar narrative trajectory.

If the first objection to the abrupt ending is that it lacks literary precedent, the second is that it lacks grammatical precedent. Of particular importance is the final sentence of Mark's Gospel: "They [the women] said nothing to anyone, for they were afraid" (16:8). While this English translation is acceptable, it should be noted that it reorders the language of the Greek text. The final word of the abrupt ending—and thus Mark's Gospel—is the conjunction γάρ or "for." It has often been suggested that sentences, paragraphs, and books do not end with conjunctions. Therefore, Mark 16:8 should not be regarded as the final verse of the narrative since it defies grammatical practice.

As was the case with the previous objection, the premise of this argument is, generally speaking, correct. Most sentences, paragraphs, and books do not end with a conjunction. But to conclude from this that no sentence, paragraph, or book can end with a conjunction goes too far. Once again, there are examples in the Bible. Several passages in the LXX (i.e., the Greek translation of the OT) evidence this construction (LXX Gen 14:3; Isa 16:10; 29:11). Perhaps the most notable example occurs in Gen 18:15 when Sarah who is advanced in age and barren laughs at the thought that she will give birth to a son. What is striking is that when Sarah is confronted about her response, she denies it "for she was afraid" (ἐφοβήθη γάρ [Gen 18:15]). The expression is particularly interesting since it is very similar to Mark 16:8 (ἐφοβοῦντο γάρ).

Along with these biblical examples, there are many examples of the construction in Greco-Roman literature. In fact, from the third century BCE to the second century CE there are 272 occurrences involving 56 different authors. Most of these examples come at the end of sentences within broader units of thought. However, as far back as 1972, P. W. van der Horst demonstrated that the construction also concludes larger segments—in this case, the thirty-second treatise of Plotinus.[10] In addition, further research has shown that γάρ concluding sentences occur across a range of genres, including narrative literature.[11] Thus, while it may be uncommon for an author to conclude a sentence, paragraph, or book with a conjunction, it is not without parallel. At the very least, a general practice does not always make for an absolute principle.

When all the evidence is considered, the abrupt ending provides the most satisfactory explanation of the data. Several variants extend the story beyond the women's response in 16:8, but these traditions are the work of later scribes who sought to ease the tension of Mark's ending. Though the conclusion to Mark's narrative is shocking and unusual, it is not without literary or grammatical precedent and likely reflects the original conclusion to the second Gospel. Having considered possible explanations of the manuscript evidence, we now turn to the interpretation of Mark's abrupt ending.

INTERPRETING THE ABRUPT ENDING

In the course of scholarly discussion, there have been four primary interpretations of Mark's abrupt ending. Each affirms that the author concluded the Gospel at 16:8 and each assumes that the ending is a deliberate strategy that invites audience participation. After this, the commonality ends. The four perspectives are significantly different and reflect

10. Van der Horst, "Can a Book End with ΓΑΡ?"
11. Iverson, "Further Word."

unique interpretations of Mark's ending as well as the wider narrative project that Mark has constructed. Each approach will be considered below along with some brief reflections.

(1) Positive Response

In the final verse of Mark's Gospel, the women flee from the tomb and say nothing to anyone. This response seems uncomplicated on the surface, but the issue is how to interpret the women's actions. Is the response a negative reaction to the angelic command? Or is it an indication of something more positive? For those adopting the first approach, the final verse of Mark's Gospel reflects a positive and somewhat expected response to the angelic encounter.

Validation for this perspective, it is argued, comes from recognizing that the concept of fear falls within the broader domain of wonder.[12] When individuals are confronted by divine revelation or the miraculous, they often respond in perplexing and mysterious ways. Such reactions are not necessarily negative, but typical of those overcome by a spiritual experience or divine encounter. For example, in Mark 9:2–8, a glorified Jesus, along with Elijah and Moses, appears before Peter, James, and John. In response to the revelatory moment, Peter offers to build three tabernacles. The proposal is quickly rebuked, but not before the narrator indicates that Peter did not know what to say because he was afraid (9:6). In this context, Peter's response is not an indictment against his character but an established and predictable reaction to the divine.

In a similar fashion, the women's response in 16:8 is not an act of disobedience or indication of a spiritual deficiency. Rather, their fear and flight are a dramatic indication that a miraculous event has taken place—in this

12. Catchpole, "Fearful Silence"; Dwyer, *Motif of Wonder.*

case, the resurrection of Jesus. As with other expressions of wonder, the response highlights a supernatural encounter that transcends the natural order. Eventually, of course, the women did fulfill the angelic command. Their initial response is intended to accentuate that, despite having been put to death, Jesus has triumphed over the grave and has been vindicated by God.

This view is attractive in many respects since it attempts to situate the women's response within a wider frame of reference, but some have questioned whether it reads too much into the Markan context. At issue is how Mark understands the concept of fear. Many have argued that fear is a pejorative term in Mark that "does not depict a proper response of faith."[13] In 5:1–20, for example, when the townspeople discover that Jesus has healed a man with a "legion" of demons, they become afraid (5:15). The reaction is difficult to classify as a positive response since the townspeople beg Jesus to leave the region (5:17), thereby indicating a rejection of his presence and ministry. For the people of the region, it is more tolerable to live with a demon-possessed man than to deal with the economic impact of Jesus's actions. Though a singular example, this illustrates what many regard as Mark's typical use of fear-related terminology. Rather than depicting a natural response to the divine, the term has more negative overtones throughout the narrative.

It is also argued that the women's response must be understood within the broader context of the narrative. Specifically, the women's flight recalls the disciples' flight in 14:50. In both scenes, Mark uses the same Greek term (φεύγω [14:50; 16:8]) to describe the followers of Jesus. The parallels are important and are an interpretive cue for the audience. Immediately after the disciples take flight, there

13. Lincoln, "Promise and the Failure," 286.

is a curious note about a man fleeing naked (14:51–52). Though bizarre, the cameo provides implicit commentary on the disciples. Similar to the anonymous man, the disciples' response is a shameful act that echoes throughout the remainder of the story. When the women flee the tomb in 16:8, not only does their fear cast a negative shadow over the scene, but their flight—and the implicit link to the disciples in 14:50—reinforces this interpretation. The women's disobedience recalls the actions of the disciples and is a negative response to the angelic messenger.

(2) Negative Response

Given the critique of the previous view, it follows that some regard the women's response as a complete failure. There is nothing positive or redeeming about the encounter. The final verses are thoroughly negative and are intended to make an important theological point: the disciples were never reunited with Jesus or commissioned to go and preach the good news to the nations.[14]

For proponents of this approach, the women's response is closely aligned with the fate of the disciples. The narrative begins by presenting the disciples in a favorable light, but quickly changes. The once responsive and faith-filled disciples soon become obstinate, faithless, and hard-hearted. As the narrative progresses, the characterization intensifies and, by the end of the story, the disciples have abandoned Jesus altogether. The only hope for redemption rests in the hands of those who have gone to the tomb where Jesus was buried. However, the women's response to the angelic messenger undermines any chance for restoration. Their fear

14. Tyson, "Blindness of the Disciples"; Weeden, *Mark*; Crossan, "Mark and the Relatives of Jesus"; Kelber, *Kingdom in Mark*.

and flight seal the fate of the disciples and terminate any opportunity for reconciliation in Galilee.

It seems reasonable to ask why Mark concluded the Gospel on this tragic note of failure. Those advancing this perspective suggest that the narrative reflects the situation of the Markan church and is intended to provide theological guidance. In this two-level drama, the unusually harsh and negative depiction is designed to undermine the authority of the disciples in the community. As such, the narrative parallels the situation of the community and its ongoing polemic against the disciples. Numerous rationales have been put forth to explain the conflict, including the idea that the disciples represent a conservative Jerusalem church or a heretical "divine-man" Christology.[15] In either case, the rejection of the disciples signifies a rejection of the community's theological adversaries. The ending provides theological justification against those antagonizing the Markan community.

While this view takes seriously the negative implications of v. 8, it goes too far in the characterization of the disciples. The disciples are dim-witted, confused, and lacking in faith. But to assume that this implies a complete rejection of the disciples is difficult to accept. Though the disciples abandon Jesus (14:50), nowhere does Jesus abandon the disciples. Even after they demonstrate (repeatedly) a lack of understanding (8:31–33; 9:31–32; 10:32–35), they are never dismissed or placed on the sidelines. Jesus continues

15. At one time it was argued that the concept of a "divine-man," or individual who possessed supernatural wisdom and power, was a thoroughly Hellenistic concept. Some scholars argued that Mark appropriated the concept of a "divine-man" in the presentation of Jesus (Bultmann, *Theology of the New Testament*). Others, however, suggested that Mark's Gospel was a polemic against a "divine-man" theology—a christological corrective that instead emphasized Jesus's suffering and death (Weeden, *Mark*).

to associate with the disciples throughout the narrative. And it is in the midst of their struggle that Jesus describes a future ministry for the disciples (13:8–13). The final scene of Mark's Gospel might be negative, but the narrative holds out hope for a future reunion (14:27–28). Indeed, if the Markan Jesus has not rejected the disciples, why should the interpreter? It seems that this decidedly negative approach runs against the logic of the narrative.

In part, this interpretation of Mark's ending is grounded in an assumed mode of communication. Many scholars have unwittingly interpreted Mark utilizing the same reading strategies employed by individuals in the twenty-first century (see ch. 5). The shortcoming of this approach is that it fails to appreciate how individuals typically experienced ancient narratives, and it ignores important distinctions between reading and performance. Because performance is a live event, the performer/audience relationship has the potential of creating experiential dynamics that are different from a typical reading event. Performance is an evocative and emotional experience by which characters are brought to life through the storytelling event. As the narrative unfolds, audiences experience emotional responses to characters, which inform their understanding of the narrative.[16] While these dynamics are complicated, audiences may develop empathetic/sympathetic feelings for characters that are extremely difficult to sever. In some cases, an audience may recognize a moral or spiritual deficiency while remaining positively disposed toward a character. Thus, although Mark's characterization may be harsh, the dynamics of performance do not demand that an audience disassociate from the disciples. To suggest that they experience terminal failure ignores Jesus's ongoing relationship with

---

16. Iverson, *Performing Early Christian Literature*.

the disciples, as well as how audiences become attached to characters in performance.

(3) Apostolic Commission

Still other interpreters push the conversation in another direction, arguing that the concluding verses are designed to function as an apostolic commission for the reader/audience. This view lays particular emphasis on the idea that Mark's ending is open and unfulfilled. The intentional gap is a rhetorical device whereby the audience is invited to complete the story by picking up where the characters failed.

Advocates of this perspective argue that Mark's ending is a "narrative trap" that plays off the depiction of the disciples and the minor characters.[17] The trap is predicated on an understanding of the disciples that is decidedly negative, though not terminal. The disciples initially respond to Jesus in faith and obedience, but they are progressively cast in a more unfavorable light as the narrative progresses. When the disciples abandon Jesus (14:50), the interpreter is not unprepared. The response is predictable given the development of the narrative. However, the disciples' desertion is not merely to accentuate their unfavorable characterization. Equally important is the narrative trap that is set for the reader/audience by Mark's plotting of the narrative.

As the disciples exit the narrative, the minor characters fill the void left by their departure. Unlike the disciples of John who care and provide for their deceased teacher (6:29), the disciples of Jesus are nowhere to be found during or after the crucifixion. Instead, it is the minor characters who take center stage. Simon of Cyrene carries Jesus's cross

17. Hester, "Dramatic Inconclusion." See also Danove, "Characterization and Narrative Function"; Tolbert, *Sowing the Gospel.*

(15:21), a group of women are present at his death (15:40–41), the centurion overseeing the crucifixion declares Jesus to be the Son of God (15:39), Joseph of Arimathea petitions Pilate for Jesus's body and buries him (15:43–46), and Mary Magdalene, Mary the mother of James, and Salome come to the tomb to anoint Jesus (16:1). Both in word and deed it is the minor characters who demonstrate their commitment to Jesus in his time of need.

Even more broadly, the minor characters are consistently portrayed in a positive fashion throughout Mark's Gospel. Though they appear for only a flashing moment, it is the minor characters who frequently embody the kind of faith and obedience that is all too often lacking among the Twelve (e.g., Mark 2:1–12; 3:31–35; 5:21–43; 7:24–30; 9:14–27; 10:46–52; 12:41–44; 14:3–9). In various ways and contexts, the minor characters model what it means to be a disciple of Jesus. This persistent and positive portrayal is in sharp contrast to the depiction of the Twelve who have been called by Jesus (3:14) and given the "mystery of the kingdom" (4:11). This tension between character groups is carefully crafted, deliberately deployed, and the catalyst for Mark's narrative trap.

When the interpreter comes to the end of Mark's Gospel, the surprise is not that the disciples have abandoned Jesus. The jolting effect of Mark's ending is that the minor characters respond in a similar fashion. Despite the favorable depiction throughout much of the narrative—extending even through the passion—the portrayal is undercut by a single, concluding verse: "And they said nothing to anyone, for they were afraid" (16:8). This act of disobedience presents an unexpected twist that leaves the audience and the narrative unsettled. The real shock of Mark's ending is that even the minor characters conclude on a note of failure.

But if the minor characters have failed to pass along the angelic command, who then will complete the narrative? Who will carry the message forward? For proponents of this approach, the conclusion is an invitation. Since all the characters have failed, it is the reader/audience who must intervene and become a witness to the world. The end of Mark's Gospel is a creative storytelling technique to draw the audience into the story—indeed to finish the story. It is an implicit apostolic commission (cf. Matt 28:18–20; Luke 24:46–69; John 21:15–23) that calls the reader/audience to complete the narrative by becoming an ideal disciple. Since the characters have failed, it is the reader/audience who must go and tell the message of Jesus's resurrection.

While this interpretation takes seriously the role of the reader/audience in the meaning-making process, it is hampered by two issues. First, although the approach attempts to explain the openness of Mark's ending, it does not account for the details of the text. The angelic command in 16:7 is to tell the disciples and Peter that Jesus is going ahead of them to Galilee. This does not appear to be a generalized call to gospel proclamation nor a summons to Christlike obedience. Further still, how is the reader/audience to communicate with individuals (i.e., the disciples and Peter) who have long since passed away? Attractive though it may be, to suggest that Mark's ending is an apostolic commission obscures the language of the text and ignores the particularities of Mark's ending.

The second problem is that the approach is beset by an internal contradiction. On the one hand, it assumes that the disciples and minor characters are depicted in a less than exemplary fashion. On the other hand, it assumes that the interpreter can complete the story. But herein lies the problem. By the end of the narrative, the minor characters (represented by the women in 16:1–8) find themselves in a state that is no different than the disciples'. Just as the disciples have failed, so too have the minor characters. In view of this pessimistic anthropological perspective and emphasis on human failure, it is not entirely clear what distinguishes the experience of the reader/audience. How is the reader/audience any different from the characters in the story? Is there any hope that the interpreter will succeed where others have failed? The trap of Mark's ending is that the interpreter faces the same predicament as the characters and, therefore, is in no position to complete the story. In sum, the details of the text and the logic of the narrative raise important questions that undermine the persuasiveness of this interpretation.

(4) Promise and Failure

Three interpretations of Mark's ending have been considered. One suggests that the women's response is positive. Another argues that Mark's ending is entirely negative and without redemption. The third proposes that the ending is a rhetorical device, designed to call the reader/audience to carry on the teaching and message of Jesus. Each of the views is intriguing in certain respects, but none has the explanatory power to account for the entirety of Mark's Gospel.

The final interpretation offers perhaps the most complete account of Mark's narrative dynamics. Proponents of this view suggest that the ending accentuates two particular themes: promise and failure.[18] The latter theme has already been noted in detail and, except for the first interpretation, is a prominent feature in each of the proposals. The women's actions, when appreciated against the narrative backdrop, reflect a negative response to the angelic command.

18. Lincoln, "Promise and the Failure."

The women (and minor characters) replace the disciples in the final chapters of the Gospel—anointing Jesus's body for burial (14:3–9), observing the crucifixion (15:40) and burial (15:47), and visiting the tomb (16:1–2)—but their fear and flight parallel the response of the Twelve. The narrative does not conclude on a note of spiritual accomplishment for either the women or the disciples.

In addition to this observation, there is a deeper irony at work in Mark's ending. The women's response is similar to a scene at the beginning of the narrative that is often identified with Mark's messianic secret (see ch. 5). In that episode (1:40–45) Jesus heals a man with leprosy and instructs him to "say nothing to anyone" (1:41). Interestingly, the command in 1:41 is very similar to the women's response in 16:8, particularly in the Greek text ("they said nothing to anyone"). Although 1:41 is a command, while 16:8 is a response to a command, it is as though the women's actions at the end of the narrative reflect their obedience to an injunction issued at the beginning of the narrative.

But this is the irony, or perhaps the double irony. While secrecy is a common feature of the narrative (1:34, 41, 44; 3:12; 5:43; 7:36; 8:26, 30; 9:9), as Jesus descends the Mount of Transfiguration, he instructs his disciples that the secret to his identity will no longer be required after the resurrection (9:9). In view of this temporal injunction, it seems as though the women have it backwards. Although some disobey the command to remain silent during Jesus's ministry (1:45; 7:36), the women fail by remaining silent after the resurrection. Despite the fact that now is the time for proclamation, emphasized by the angelic command to "go and tell" (16:7), the women flee in silence, thereby intensifying the theme of failure.

However, the theme of failure, prominent though it may be, is not the only feature of Mark's ending. Equally

as important is the promise in 16:7. Though many interpreters focus on a single aspect of 16:7—the instruction to
"go and tell"—attention is also placed on the reunion with
the disciples: "[H]e is going before you to Galilee; *there you
will see him, just as he told you*" (16:7, emphasis added).
The latter portion of this statement is often overlooked and
must be held in tandem with the women's response in 16:8.
By and large, 16:7 is a summary of Jesus's words in 14:28.
There, in the context of the Passover meal, Jesus instructs
the disciples that they will fall away but that he "will go" before them to Galilee. This promise is carried forward to the
empty tomb scene when the angelic messenger reiterates
Jesus's original statement to the disciples. While the command to "go and tell" is disobeyed, the interpreter should
not assume that the anticipated reunion with the disciples
has been foiled.

Why? Because the promise in 16:7 is linked to the
character of Jesus. And quite simply, Jesus is not like the
other earthly characters in the narrative. His word has power, "authority" (e.g., 1:22, 27), and it "will not pass away"
(13:31). The certainty of his word is illustrated in various
predictions throughout the narrative. For example, Jesus
rightly predicts where the disciples will find a colt that is
used for his entry into Jerusalem (11:2–7), the location of
the Passover meal (14:13–16), Judas's betrayal (14:18–21,
43–45), and Peter's denials (14:30, 66–72), as well as his
own death and resurrection (8:31; 9:31; 10:32–34). In each
instance, Jesus is proven trustworthy as his prophetic word
is brought to fruition.

The anticipated reunion in Galilee (14:28; 16:7) is
therefore not the only prediction in Mark's narrative and
must be interpreted against the broader portrait of Jesus.
Because Jesus is a reliable character whose word is true, the
promise of restoration will be fulfilled. How and when it

will be accomplished is not described in the narrative. But the audience knows that somehow, someway, the reunion will be accomplished. The audience expects this *because Jesus predicted it*. The reunion with the disciples is not dependent on any character in the narrative except Jesus. If Jesus can predict the circumstances surrounding his own death and resurrection, certainly he can foretell a regathering with his fallible followers.[19]

The final question is why Mark punctuates the narrative by stressing promise and failure. How is the interpreter to understand this conclusion? Proponents argue that the narrative design emphasizes important theological themes—in this case, discipleship and Christology. Mark's ending reflects pastoral sensibilities that underscore the challenge for all would-be followers (see ch. 4). The narrative makes no attempt, either at the beginning, middle, or end, to gloss over the struggle of being a disciple. It does not paint a fantastical portrait of the Christian life complete with unicorns and rainbows. Mark's story is a reminder that all are called, but no one finds it easy.[20] The burdens of earthly existence, suffering and persecution, trials and strife, even failure, are part of the Christian experience. As the women failed at the empty tomb, so too have all disciples failed both within and beyond the narrative.

But in the midst of this stark and honest assessment, Mark nonetheless offers a message of "good news" (1:1). The same God who raised and vindicated Jesus (16:6) will also raise and vindicate the follower of Jesus. The ending is an invitation for fragile disciples to reflect on the promises of

19. The writing of the second Gospel is implicit witness that the women's silence was not permanent and that the promise of a reunion was fulfilled. The expression "fallible followers" derives from Malbon, *In the Company of Jesus*, 41–69.

20. Malbon, *In the Company of Jesus*, 67.

God. Because God never fails, "[t]he conclusion to Mark's Gospel is not a message of failure, but a resounding affirmation of God's design to overcome all imaginable human failure (16:1–8)" through his beloved Son.[21] The narrative offers reassurance that God's love persists even when the followers of Jesus do not, that God triumphs over all human failure, and that the end of Mark's story is not the end of the Gospel. The enigmatic conclusion is a powerful reminder that human failure will not have the final word in God's redemptive plan.

Table 6.2			
Interpretations of the Abrupt Ending (Mark 16:8)			
Positive Response	**Negative Response**	**Apostolic Commission**	**Promise & Failure**
· The women respond as expected after a divine encounter. · The women were shell-shocked, and their fear/flight was only temporary.	· All disciples (men and women) fail. · Polemic against the disciples is based on a situation within the Markan community. · Audience is to distance themselves from the failed disciples.	· Mark's ending is a "narrative trap." · Disciples and minor characters fail. · Audience is to pick up where the followers of Jesus left off by proclaiming Jesus's resurrection.	· All disciples (men and women) fail. · The promise of a reunion in Galilee is fulfilled in accord with Jesus's word. · God overcomes all human failure.

21. Moloney, *Gospel of Mark*, 354.

CONCLUSION

Mark's ending is fascinating, frustrating, and provocative. It is fascinating because it brings together discussion from various perspectives (historical, textual, and literary). It is frustrating because the evidence is fragmentary and non-conclusive. And it is provocative because it invites the interpreter to piece together data in creative and diverse ways, evidenced by the rich history of scholarly discussion.

For well over a millennium the longer ending was regarded as an authentic conclusion to Mark's Gospel, but many scholars now embrace the abrupt ending. In the wake of this shift in scholarly opinion, a number of interpretations have been suggested. Though the perspectives differ, they all share an underlying assumption about the interpretive process. Each requires the interpreter to become a participant in the narrative. And each requires the interpreter to imagine or become something beyond the story world of Mark's Gospel. What the interpreter is to infer specifically from Mark's truncated ending is an ongoing debate. What can be affirmed, however, is that Mark's conclusion reflects a creative storyteller who sought to speak to the ongoing realities of the Markan community and beyond.

QUESTIONS FOR REFLECTION

1. On your own, read through the conclusions in Matthew, Luke, and John. Compare and contrast these endings to Mark's Gospel.

2. Which explanation of Mark's abrupt ending do you find most persuasive? Why?

FURTHER READING

Catchpole, David. "The Fearful Silence of the Women at the Tomb: A Study in Markan Theology." *Journal of Theology for Southern Africa* 18 (1977) 3–10.

Croy, N. Clayton. *The Mutilation of Mark's Gospel.* Nashville: Abingdon, 2003.

Danove, Paul. "The Characterization and Narrative Function of the Women at the Tomb (Mark 15,40–41.47; 16,1–8)." *Bib* 77 (1996) 375–97.

Dwyer, Timothy. *The Motif of Wonder in the Gospel of Mark.* JSNTSup 128. Sheffield: Sheffield Academic, 1996.

Hester, J. David. "Dramatic Inconclusion: Irony and the Narrative Rhetoric of the Ending of Mark." *JSNT* 57 (1995) 61–86.

Hooker, Morna D. *Endings: Invitations to Discipleship.* Peabody, MA: Hendrickson, 2003.

Iverson, Kelly R. "A Further Word on Final Γάρ (Mark 16:8)." *CBQ* 68 (2006) 79–94.

———. "A Postmodern Riddle? Gaps, Inferences and Mark's Abrupt Ending." *JSNT* 44 (2022) 337–67.

Lincoln, Andrew T. "The Promise and the Failure: Mark 16:7, 8." *JBL* 108 (1989) 283–300.

Lunn, Nicholas P. *The Original Ending of Mark: A New Case for the Authenticity of Mark 16:9–20.* Eugene, OR: Pickwick Publications, 2014.

Magness, J. Lee. *Sense and Absence: Structure and Suspension in the Ending of Mark's Gospel.* Semeia Studies. Atlanta: Scholars, 1986.

Metzger, Bruce M. *A Textual Commentary on the Greek New Testament.* 2nd ed. New York: United Bible Societies, 1994.

Tyson, Joseph B. "The Blindness of the Disciples in Mark." *JBL* 80 (1961) 261–68.

Van der Horst, P. W. "Can a Book End with ΓΑΡ? A Note on Mark XVI.8." *JTS* 23 (1972) 121–24.

Weeden, Theodore J. *Mark: Traditions in Conflict.* Philadelphia: Fortress, 1971.

SELECT BIBLIOGRAPHY

Bauckham, Richard. *The Gospels for All Christians: Rethinking the Gospel Audiences*. Grand Rapids: Eerdmans, 1998.

Beavis, Mary Ann. *Mark*. Paideia. Grand Rapids: Baker, 2011.

Best, Ernest. *Following Jesus: Discipleship in the Gospel of Mark*. JSNTSup 4. Sheffield: JSOT Press, 1981.

———. *Mark: The Gospel as Story*. Edinburgh: T. & T. Clark, 1983.

Bird, Michael F. *Jesus among the Gods: Early Christology in the Greco-Roman World*. Waco, TX: Baylor University Press, 2022.

Boomershine, Thomas E. *First-Century Gospel Storytellers and Audiences: The Gospels as Performance Literature*. BPCS 17. Eugene, OR: Cascade Books, 2022.

———. *The Messiah of Peace: A Performance-Criticism Commentary on Mark's Passion-Resurrection Narrative*. BPCS 12. Eugene, OR: Cascade Books, 2015.

Boring, M. Eugene. *Mark: A Commentary*. NTL. Louisville: Westminster John Knox, 2006.

Brown, Jeannine K. *Gospels as Stories: A Narrative Approach to Matthew, Mark, Luke, and John*. Grand Rapids: Baker, 2020.

Bultmann, Rudolf. *Theology of the New Testament*. Translated by Kendrick Grobel. 2 vols. New York: Scribner, 1951 55.

Burridge, Richard A. *What Are the Gospels? A Comparison with Graeco-Roman Biography*. SNTSMS 70. Cambridge: Cambridge University Press, 1992.

Catchpole, David. "The Fearful Silence of the Women at the Tomb: A Study in Markan Theology." *Journal of Theology for Southern Africa* 18 (1977) 3–10.

Collins, Adela Yarbro. *Mark: A Commentary*. Hermeneia. Minneapolis: Fortress, 2007.

———. "Mark's Interpretation of the Death of Jesus." *JBL* 128 (2009) 545–54.

Collins, Nancy L., and Lynn Carol Miller. "Self-Disclosure and Liking: A Meta-Analytic Review." *Psychological Bulletin* 116 (1994) 457–75.

Combs, Jason Robert. "A Ghost on the Water? Understanding an Absurdity in Mark 6:49–50." *JBL* 127 (2008) 345–58.

Crossan, John Dominic. "Mark and the Relatives of Jesus." *NovT* 15 (1973) 81–113.

Croy, N. Clayton. *The Mutilation of Mark's Gospel.* Nashville: Abingdon, 2003.

Culpepper, R. Alan. *Mark.* Smyth & Helwys Bible Commentary. Macon, GA: Smyth & Helwys, 2007.

Danove, Paul. "The Characterization and Narrative Function of the Women at the Tomb (Mark 15,40–41.47; 16,1–8)." *Bib* 77 (1996) 375–97.

Depew, Mary, and Dirk Obbink. *Matrices of Genre: Authors, Canons, and Society.* Cambridge: Harvard University Press, 2000.

Dewey, Joanna. "Mark as Interwoven Tapestry: Forecasts and Echoes for a Listening Audience." *CBQ* 53 (1991) 221–36.

Disney (illustrator). *Pooh's Best Day: A Book about Weather.* Baby's First Disney Books. Danbury, CT: Grolier, 2006.

Donahue, John R., and Daniel J. Harrington. *The Gospel of Mark.* SP 2. Collegeville, MN: Liturgical, 2002.

Dwyer, Timothy. *The Motif of Wonder in the Gospel of Mark.* JSNTSup 128. Sheffield: Sheffield Academic, 1996.

Edwards, James R. "Markan Sandwiches: The Significance of Interpolations in Markan Narratives." *NovT* (1989) 193–216.

Evans, Craig A. *Mark 8:27—16:20.* WBC 34B. Dallas: Word, 2001.

Farmer, William. *The Last Twelve Verses of Mark.* Cambridge: Cambridge University Press, 1974.

Focant, Camille. *The Gospel According to Mark: A Commentary.* Translated by Leslie Robert Keylock. Eugene, OR: Pickwick, 2012.

Fowler, Robert M. *Let the Reader Understand: Reader-Response Criticism and the Gospel of Mark.* Minneapolis: Fortress, 1991.

———. "Why Everything We Know about the Bible Is Wrong: Lessons from the Media History of the Bible." In *The Bible in Ancient and Modern Media,* edited by Holly E. Hearon and Philip Ruge-Jones, 3–18. BPCS 1. Eugene, OR: Cascade Books, 2009.

France, R. T. *The Gospel of Mark: A Commentary on the Greek Text.* NIGTC. Grand Rapids: Eerdmans, 2002.

Gamel, Brian K. *Mark 15:39 as a Markan Theology of Revelation: The Centurion's Confession as Apocalyptic Unveiling.* LNTS 574. London: Bloomsbury, 2017.

Geddert, Timothy J. "The Implied YHWH Christology of Mark's Gospel: Mark's Challenge to the Reader to 'Connect the Dots.'" *BBR* 25 (2015) 325–40.

Gibson, Jeffrey B. "The Rebuke of the Disciples in Mark 8:14–21." *JSNT* 27 (1986) 31–47.

Guelich, Robert A. *Mark 1—8:26.* WBC 34A. Dallas: Word, 1989.

Hester, J. David. "Dramatic Inconclusion: Irony and the Narrative Rhetoric of the Ending of Mark." *JSNT* 57 (1995) 61–86.

Hooker, Morna D. *Endings: Invitations to Discipleship.* Peabody, MA: Hendrickson, 2003.

———. *The Gospel according to Saint Mark.* BNTC. London: A&C, 1991.

Horsley, Richard A. *Hearing the Whole Story: The Politics of Plot in Mark's Gospel.* Louisville: Westminster John Knox, 2001.

Iser, Wolfgang. "The Reading Process: A Phenomenological Approach." *New Literary History* 3 (1972) 279–99.

Iverson, Kelly R. "A Centurion's 'Confession': A Performance-Critical Analysis of Mark 15:39." *JBL* 130 (2011) 329–50.

———. "A Further Word on Final Γάρ (Mark 16:8)." *CBQ* 68 (2006) 79–94.

———. *Gentiles in the Gospel of Mark: Even the Dogs under the Table Eat the Children's Crumbs.* LNTS 339. London: T. & T. Clark, 2007.

———. *Performing Early Christian Literature: Audience Experience and Interpretation of the Gospels.* Cambridge: Cambridge University Press, 2021.

———. "A Postmodern Riddle? Gaps, Inferences and Mark's Abrupt Ending." *JSNT* 44 (2022) 337–67.

———. "'Wherever the Gospel Is Preached': The Paradox of Secrecy in the Gospel of Mark." In *Mark as Story: Retrospect and Prospect*, edited by Kelly R. Iverson and Christopher W. Skinner, 181–210. Resources for Biblical Studies 65. Atlanta: SBL, 2011.

Johansson, Daniel. "Kurios in the Gospel of Mark." *JSNT* 33 (2010) 101–24.

———. "'Who Can Forgive Sins but God Alone?' Human and Angelic Agents, and Divine Forgiveness in Early Judaism." *JSNT* 33 (2011) 351–74.

Juel, Donald H. *The Gospel of Mark.* Interpreting Biblical Texts. Nashville: Abingdon, 1999.

————. *A Master of Surprise: Mark Interpreted*. Minneapolis: Fortress, 1994.

Kähler, Martin. *The So-Called Historical Jesus and the Historic Biblical Christ*. Translated, edited, and introduced by Carl E. Braaten. Philadelphia: Fortress, 1964.

Kelber, Werner H. *The Kingdom in Mark: A New Place and a New Time*. Philadelphia: Fortress, 1974.

Kingsbury, Jack Dean. *The Christology of Mark's Gospel*. Philadelphia: Fortress, 1983.

————. *Conflict in Mark: Jesus, Authorities, Disciples*. Minneapolis: Fortress, 1989.

Kirk, J. R. Daniel, ed. *Christology in Mark's Gospel: Four Views*. Critical Points. Grand Rapids: Zondervan, 2021.

————. *A Man Attested by God: The Human Jesus of the Synoptic Gospels*. Grand Rapids: Eerdmans, 2016.

Lincoln, Andrew T. "The Promise and the Failure: Mark 16:7, 8." *JBL* 108 (1989) 283–300.

Lunn, Nicholas P. *The Original Ending of Mark: A New Case for the Authenticity of Mark 16:9–20*. Eugene, OR: Pickwick Publications, 2014.

Luz, Ulrich. "The Secrecy Motif and the Marcan Christology." In *The Messianic Secret*, edited by Christopher Tuckett, 75–96. IRT 1. Philadelphia: Fortress, 1983.

Magness, J. Lee. *Sense and Absence: Structure and Suspension in the Ending of Mark's Gospel*. Semeia Studies. Atlanta: Scholars, 1986.

Malbon, Elizabeth Struthers. *Hearing Mark: A Listener's Guide*. Harrisburg, PA: Trinity, 2002.

————. "History, Theology, Story: Re-Contextualizing Mark's 'Messianic Secret.'" In *Character Studies and the Gospel of Mark*, edited by Christopher W. Skinner and Matthew Ryan Hauge, 35–56. LNTS 483. London: Bloomsbury, 2014.

————. *In the Company of Jesus: Characters in Mark's Gospel*. Louisville: Westminster John Knox, 2000.

————. *Mark's Jesus: Characterization as Narrative Christology*. Waco, TX: Baylor University Press, 2009.

————. *Narrative Space and Mythic Meaning in Mark*. New Voices in Biblical Studies. San Francisco: Harper & Row, 1986.

Malbon, Elizabeth Struthers, and Sharyn Dowd. "The Significance of Jesus' Death in Mark: Narrative Context and Authorial Audience." *JBL* 125 (2006) 271–97.

Marcus, Joel. *Mark 1–8: A New Translation with Introduction and Commentary*. AB 27. New York: Doubleday, 2000.

————. *Mark 8–16: A New Translation with Introduction and Commentary.* Anchor Yale Bible 27A. New Haven: Yale University Press, 2009.

————. *The Way of the Lord: Christological Exegesis of the Old Testament in the Gospel of Mark.* Louisville: Westminster John Knox, 1992.

Metzger, Bruce M. *A Textual Commentary on the Greek New Testament.* 2nd ed. New York: United Bible Societies, 1994.

Miller, Susan. *Women in Mark's Gospel.* JSNTSup 259. New York: T. & T. Clark, 2004.

Moloney, Francis J. *The Gospel of Mark: A Commentary.* Peabody, MA: Hendrickson, 2002.

Nineham, Dennis E. *St. Mark.* London: SCM, 1969.

Räisänen, Heikki. "The 'Messianic Secret' in Mark's Gospel." In *The Messianic Secret,* edited by Christopher Tuckett, 132–40. IRT 1. Philadelphia: Fortress, 1983.

Reid, Duncan. "The Significance of the 'Ransom Saying' in Mark 10:45." *CBQ* 84 (2022) 424–41.

Resseguie, James L. *Narrative Criticism of the New Testament: An Introduction.* Grand Rapids: Baker, 2005.

Rhoads, David. "Performance Criticism: An Emerging Methodology in Second Temple Studies—Part I." *Biblical Theology Bulletin* 36 (2006) 118–33.

————. "Performance Criticism: An Emerging Methodology in Second Temple Studies—Part II." *Biblical Theology Bulletin* 36 (2006) 164–84.

————. "Performance Events in Early Christianity: New Testament Writings in an Oral Context." In *The Interface of Orality and Writing: Speaking, Seeing, Writing in the Shaping of New Genres,* edited by Annette Weissenrieder and Robert B. Coote, 166–93. BPCS 11. Eugene, OR: Cascade Books, 2015.

Rhoads, David, and Joanna Dewey. "Performance Criticism: A Paradigm Shift in New Testament Studies." In *From Text to Performance: Narrative and Performance Criticisms in Dialogue and Debate,* edited by Kelly R. Iverson, 1–26. BPCS 10. Eugene, OR: Cascade Books, 2014.

Rhoads, David, et al. *Mark as Story: An Introduction to the Narrative of a Gospel.* 3rd ed. Minneapolis: Fortress, 2012.

Sanday, William. *The Life of Christ in Recent Research.* Oxford: Clarendon, 1907.

Schweitzer, Albert. *The Quest of the Historical Jesus.* Translated by W. Montgomery et al. Edited by John Bowden. Minneapolis: Fortress, 2001.

Senior, Donald. *The Passion of Jesus in the Gospel of Mark.* Collegeville, MN: Liturgical, 1991.

Shiner, Whitney Taylor. *Proclaiming the Gospel: First-Century Performance of Mark.* Harrisburg, PA: Trinity, 2003.

Shively, Elizabeth E. "Recognizing Penguins: Audience Expectation, Cognitive Genre Theory, and the Ending of Mark's Gospel." *CBQ* 80 (2018) 273–92.

Tannehill, Robert C. "The Disciples in Mark: The Function of a Narrative Role." *JR* 57 (1977) 386–405.

Tolbert, Mary Ann. *Sowing the Gospel: Mark's World in Literary-Historical Perspective.* Minneapolis: Fortress, 1989.

Troftgruben, Troy M. *A Conclusion Unhindered: A Study of the Ending of Acts within Its Literary Environment.* WUNT 2/280. Tübingen: Mohr Siebeck, 2010.

Tyson, Joseph B. "The Blindness of the Disciples in Mark." *JBL* 80 (1961) 261–68.

Van der Horst, P. W. "Can a Book End with ΓΑΡ? A Note on Mark XVI.8." *JTS* 23 (1972) 121–24.

Van Iersel, Bas M. F. *Mark: A Reader-Response Commentary.* Translated by W. H. Bisscheroux. JSNTSup 164. Sheffield: Sheffield Academic, 1998.

Watson, David F. *Honor among Christians: The Cultural Key to the Messianic Secret.* Minneapolis: Fortress, 2010.

Watts, Rikki E. *Isaiah's New Exodus in Mark.* WUNT 88. Tübingen: Mohr Siebeck, 1997.

Weeden, Theodore J. *Mark: Traditions in Conflict.* Philadelphia: Fortress, 1971.

Whitenton, Michael R. "Feeling the Silence: A Moment-by-Moment Account of Emotions at the End of Mark (16:1–8)." *CBQ* 78 (2016) 272–89.

———. *Hearing Kyriotic Sonship: A Cognitive and Rhetorical Approach to the Characterization of Mark's Jesus.* BIS 148. Leiden: Brill, 2016.

Williams, Joel F. "Literary Approaches to the End of Mark's Gospel." *JETS* 42 (1999) 21–35.

———. *Other Followers of Jesus: Minor Characters as Major Figures in Mark's Gospel.* JSNTSup 102. Sheffield: JSOT Press, 1994.

Winn, Adam. *Reading Mark's Christology under Caesar: Jesus the Messiah and the Roman Imperial Ideology*. Downers Grove, IL: InterVarsity, 2018.

———. "Resisting Honor: The Markan Secrecy Motif and Roman Political Ideology." *JBL* 133 (2014) 583–601.

Wrede, William. *The Messianic Secret*. Translated by J. C. G. Greig. Library of Theological Translations. Cambridge: James Clarke, 1971.